INTELLIGENT
DESIGN
VS.
EVOLUTION

INTELLIGENT
DESIGN
VS.
EVOLUTION

Letters to an Atheist

RAY COMFORT

Bridge-Logos
Orlando, Florida 32822

Bridge-Logos

Orlando, FL 32822 USA

Intelligent Design vs. Evolution
by Ray Comfort

Printed in the United States of America.

Library of Congress Catalog Card Number: 2006924641
International Standard Book Number 0-88270-166-5

Unless otherwise indicated, Scriptures in this book are from the *King James Version* of the Bible.

G1.316.N.m604.352100

Foreword

When James David Franz first wrote to me back in 1998, he asked why I didn't accept the "scientific facts" that support evolution. I wrote back a quote note saying that there was more proof that the earth was flat. That didn't amuse him.

I normally don't have time to write back and forth to atheists, but this man seemed to be an interesting character. Over a few months of correspondence, I collected our emails, thinking that they might one day make an interesting book. Then I forgot about them.

Seven years later, I received an email from a woman who had read one of his most powerful letters, one that I had published in *The Evidence Bible*,[1] and she asked how I had responded to it. I searched for the file, found my reply, and read it. I remembered how interesting this correspondence had been.

Here, now, is the interaction between James Franz and me. So that you will know who is who, the font in which James writes is "plain," and my font is "**bold**." I'll clarify this for you as the letters begin and you can see them.

The issues we discussed concern all of us, so I have provided detailed, footnoted commentary beside our conversation for you in the column on the outside edge of each page. I want you to understand my responses, so that you, too, will have references and foundations from which to draw when you discuss intelligent design vs. evolution.

I invite you now into a conversation that was heated, amusing, stimulating, and enlightening, and one that I hope will deepen your ability to engage in similar debates.

Sincerely,

Ray Comfort

E volution is a "faith." It's what you believe to be true ... no evidence ... just monkey skulls, etc. Try and prove the earth is flat. There's more evidence for that.

"The soul that sins, it shall die." Everything degenerates. It dies. It's called "entropy," a fact that proves evolution to be a theory tale.[1]

I'd like to see your evidence for the flat Earth, I'm sure it would be very intriguing. And you say "no evidence ... just monkey skulls, etc." You are so idiotic ... That's like living in the city and saying, "There's no evidence for trees, just wood, etc." You say it like you're simply laughing, because the phrase "monkey skulls" sounds funny. It does sound funny. Maybe I'll start a little comic book called, "Monkey Skulls," which teaches children about evolution, and put it into "tracts" and pass them out just outside of churches.[2] Would you like that? It would be more than fair. If you've never actually looked at the comparisons of monkey skulls and human skulls, and you have no other way of explaining the incredible number of similarities (I'm going to put together a list of them for you, and pictures!), then you have no room to discount the evidence.[3] Maybe you

[1] Mr. Franz's words are in regular type. Mine are in boldface. When Mr. Franz and I quote each other, the words are within << >>.

[2] This is a reference to the gospel tracts, specifically "The Atheist Test": www.livingwaters.com. Click on "store," "Gospel tracts," then "Atheist test."

[3] The reason for the similarity of the skulls of apes and humans is addressed in the DVD, "The Science of Evolution." This is available through www.livingwaters.com.

4 In Ralph Epperson's book, *The Unseen Hand* (1985-01, Publius Press), he stated that the world had approximately 4 billion people (now closer to five). If you took the population of the world, split it up into families of four and gave them each a piece of land 50' x 53', the entire population of the planet would fit neatly into the state of Oregon. In Mary Pride's book, *The Way Home* (Crossway), she calculated that you could give every person in the world 2,000 square feet (which is larger than most homes) and everyone would fit into the state of Texas. If you don't believe this, take a flight from Los Angeles to New York. Make sure you get a window seat, and sit for hours staring out of the window at the millions upon millions of acres of land without a hint of human habitation.

Holland for instance is the most heavily populated country in Europe, with an average density of 1.84 people per acre, which is the same as an area of 1,423 square yards (a plot 37.5 yards {34.25 m} square) for each man, woman, child and baby living in Holland today. This is quite a bit more than most of them own at the moment. Yet Brazil, home of decimated rainforests, shanty towns the size of major European cities, some of the poorest

should try a little intellectual stimulation before you go making assumption and disregarding facts.

Anyone who doesn't think that death is a natural process is most definitely ignorant of everything that science has taught them. You, sir, are the greatest religiously blinded fool I have ever had the displeasure of debating with. Your arguments are weak, flimsy, self-contradictory, uninformed, poorly organized, badly thought out, mindless, pointless, ignorant, simple, and mind-numbingly dull. You probably think that "intellectual stimulation" is some kind of sin of the flesh or something.

You call *that* proof that evolution is false? Your line of thought is laughable at best. Everything degenerates, yes ... this is a basic scientific fact, and there are reasons for its happening. The fact that things die actually supports evolution ... it's called the "Cycle of Life," and is part of natural process, and also a tool of evolution. Nothing can go on forever, because if it did, everything would be constantly consuming, and nearly none of the chemical energy would be returning to the earth (through death). Then, there would be problems such as: no more breathable air, because all of the animals and their children and on down the line have eaten all the plants. Only pure carnivores would survive, because all herbivores would die off, because the plants wouldn't be dying and returning their energy to the earth. Of course, they'd then be dying, wouldn't they? There would be such problems without sin, just imagine it: Extreme overpopulation[4] and a ravaging of the earth's natural resources. Eventually all these righteous humans would be covering every corner of the earth, because for hundreds of years not one of them would die. See the flaws in your logic? Oh, wait, I'm sorry—you don't operate on logic. Sometimes I forget that the bible teaches ignorance.[5]

Imagine if that were to happen in only a few hundred years. Trust me, if no one died, they would cover the globe, and eventually suffocate themselves, and someone would have to die. You can free up every square inch, but that all that means is that it would take just a little longer.

Mother evolution would fix things up. Perhaps she could make another "big bang" and the earth would expand. Or perhaps she would cause everyone to shrink in size ... she's done a good job so far in creating flowers, birds, fruits, trees, seasons, the incredible human body, etc ... Nothing is too hard for God Evolution.[6]

* * *

people on earth in their teeming millions—an apparent glimpse of our possible future—has a population density of only 0.08 people per acre, giving plots of more than 817,960 square yards (827 meters square) for each individual, or areas of 676 acres for the 'average' two-parent, two child family—more than enough to live on by most peoples standards. http://www.geocities.com/RainForest/3046/overpop.htm

5 See *Scientific Facts in the Bible*, Ray Comfort (Bridge-Logos Publishers)

6 The symbols * * * denote a change of subject (which may be continued further), or a reference to a previous subject.

3

Ray, I have a real question for you. Are you baptized? Are you a faithful Christian? Do you have faith in Jesus? Do you trust Jesus and your Lord with all your heart? Do you in any way doubt your Lord? Do you believe you are good enough to receive your Lord's blessings, salvation, and love? Then take a simple test of faith. Mark 16:16-18—This is in Jesus' words: "He who believes and is baptized will be saved; but he who does not believe will be condemned. And these signs will follow those who believe ... they will take up serpents; and if they drink anything deadly, it will by no means hurt them; they will lay hands on the sick, and they will recover."

I want you to prove to me and yourself once and for all whether or not god exists. Drink a deadly dose of cyanide (or any poison you desire, as long as it is deadly, and in sufficient amount to cause death), hold your faith close to your heart, and pray if you feel the need. If the bible is as true as you say, and the words of Jesus are the words of truth, and if you believe that, then you should have no problem with this test, and you should not die. If you say this is silly, then you discount scripture and you have doubt in your heart.

If you say that you don't need to take this kind of test to prove your faith, then you fear that what you believe is not true, because in your heart you should have nothing to lose. I will even acquire whatever poison you wish me to if you do not want the burden of buying it. I will travel to where you live, and I will deliver it to you myself, and I will stay with you after you take the poison.[7] You have absolutely nothing to lose, unless you're wrong, because I am more than willing to go very far out of my way to assist you in this test. It will only take a few minutes of your time, and then I will be on my way. Certainly you can spare a few minutes. If you shrug this off, it shows doubt in your heart. If you say "that's not the true intent of that passage," then what is it? It seems clear as day to me—the word of god couldn't be more plain and easy to understand. The only reason you should turn down this test is if your faith is not strong and sincere, or if you think the bible is not true, or if you think you're not good enough for god's love. And, I am more than serious about buying poison for you and coming to your home. I will do it if you want to actually take this test.

I thought I should let you know two things: I will take any absence of a response to my query of the test of faith as evidence that you do have doubt in your bible and your god, and that your faith is not true, strong, or sincere. Thus, it is in your best interests to respond. I am trying not to pressure

7 The offering of poison to Christians (in respect to this verse) is popular with atheists. At the American Atheists, Inc. debate, atheist Mr. Frank Zindler publicly challenged me to eat a bag of poisoned peanuts. See: http://www.angelfire.com/nj2/atheists/conv2001.html.

you into threatening your life, as I am leaving the choice of taking this test completely up to you. All you need to do is let me know whether you want to take it or not. At the bottom is my legal disclaimer, please read it and understand it fully before you make a decision.

8 Permission was originally obtained to use Mr. Franz's real name. However, it hasn't been used in this publication.

Disclaimer: I, James David Franz, [8] do not intend for anything that I said to be construed as threatening to the life of Mr. Ray Comfort, or pressuring him into doing so. The choice being completely his, I will claim no influence in the final decision, and I am exempt from any criminal charges that can be pressed because of resulting harm or death from this test. I do not endorse taking any poison whatsoever, as doing so can result in hospitalization, extreme sickness, and/or death. I highly recommend that anyone who has accidentally or purposefully taken poisons or anything harmful to the body immediately seek medical attention, and induce vomiting if necessary and if safe. I claim no responsibility for the actions of Mr. Ray Comfort whether it be by his own will or as a result of my presentation of this test. I present this test only as an idea for his consideration, not as a recommendation on his part to take any poisons or threaten his life in any way whatsoever.

You, sir, are the greatest religiously blinded fool I have ever had the displeasure of debating with.

If I'm so stupid, why do you keep talking to me?

Why don't you go handle snakes? You say there are false words in the bible,[9] and since so many say it is the word of god, that must not be true. Since the bible is the only evidence (I have to really stretch to even call it that) for many religions, by your words I must infer that they are not true as well, and that the existence of god is as false as the bible, which you have just admitted. It's true—if you tout the bible as true, use it as your only source of argument, and call it the word of god, then you cannot, by your own admission, simply discount what you don't want to hear, because then you are destroying the very foundation you stand on. Where's your faith?

Why don't I just join one of those deep-thinking snake-handling churches?

So then you'll take the test? Maybe you didn't think I was serious. I am.

* * *

There was another point I've been meaning to tell to you, to point out your false logic. In your atheist test on your web page, you say that with the

[9] This statement is not true.

atheist's reasoning, when you throw oranges in the air, they should land in order (the way they were situated in your diagram). Yet, through that very argument, you are saying that the stars in the sky should be in order—maybe not as apparent of an order as your oranges, but a pattern nonetheless. I've looked at star charts and the sky, and it all seems to be random. Could you please point out to me this order?[10] I would appreciate it very much. See where your logic fails when you try to apply it to reality?

* * *

But with me, when I say "religious," I'm talking about something I call "abstract pantheism," which is the basic idea (abstract) that exists within nearly every religion (pan-): the existence of any theistic deity (theism).

That would mean that anyone with a brain is religious.

Okay, now you're mixing up arguments, which is totally fallacious. I'm pointing out the flaws in your religious views by creating a hypothetical scenario in which god exists and there is no sin, a world where everyone lives forever and there is no such thing as evolution. Then you go throwing evolution into it and making totally absurd points, such as the earth would explode into a bigger

10 All of creation, including stars may look random to the unlearned eye. For example, trees grow at random all over the face of the earth. They have been scattered by God throughout the whole planet so that we can have ready access to fruit, wood, medicines through their leaves, and to oxygenate the air (as well as enhance the landscape). God created the "star" of the sun to rule the earth by day. [See Genesis 1:16.] The sun is 93,000,000 miles away. If it were any closer or farther away, there would be no life on earth. Its position is not "random." There are innumerable worlds that seem to be scattered as tiny sparklings in the heavens, but each one has its own individual order—its moons, governing laws, placement, etc. Think of how each of how the planets in our own little Milky Way move with intricate precision around our sun.

earth. Your argumentation and logic is very tainted with uneducated and irrelevant spoutings.

Theologians such as yourself call and scream for proof, yet they don't bother to ever show any for their side of the argument, and they ignore the proof that is out there.[11] I say "I believe"[12] and "probably" because there's no way we'll ever know how the first animal walked onto land and what it looked like, because it happened millions, perhaps billions of years ago.[13] There is modern proof for evolution, and you have totally ignored my pointing it out. You say you've found the truth—prove it. I've already given you one opportunity, and you scoffed at it.

Let me tell you something I discovered—there are two things that happened at the beginnings of the earth's life that the bible does not mention as occurring, nor does it dispute them. In fact, the millions and millions of years before humankind are summed up as a few days (which in god's eyes could be millennia). These two occurrences are dinosaurs and evolution. When science found proof for the existence of dinosaurs,[14] theists had no choice but to accept it, even though the bible didn't say it happened (one example of religion giving way to scientific discovery—to truth). Now, theists are saying evolution

11 "Evolution is unproved and unprovable. We believe it only because the only alternative is special creation, and that is unthinkable." (Sir Arthur Keith, author of Foreword to *The Origin of Species*, 100th edition).

12 This is a reference to the language of "speculation," which is religiously used by believers in the theory of evolution. Because of a lack of scientific proof for the theory, they are continually forced to use words such as maybe, probably, perhaps, etc.

13 "Time" is the magic ingredient in the evolutionist's fantastic faith. For them, time makes the impossible believable.

14 The Bible not only mentions dinosaurs, it tells us why they disappeared, something science hasn't yet discovered. In Job 40:15-24 (written 3,000 BC), God Himself speaks, describing the largest of all the creatures He made. He tells of this massive animal as being herbivorous (plant-eating), having its strength in its hips, a tail like a large tree, very strong bones, a habitat among trees, able to consume large amounts of water, and being of great heights. Then the Scriptures say, "... He who made him can make his sword to approach unto himself." In other words, God brought extinction to this huge prehistoric creature. (From *The Evidence Bible* Bridge-Logos Publishers.)

15 Either evolution is true or the Bible is true. They cannot walk hand-in-hand. The Bible makes it clear that God made man in His image [see Genesis 1:26], that each animal brings forth "after its own kind" (it doesn't change species), and that animal flesh is different than human flesh—"All flesh is not the same flesh: but there is one kind of flesh for men, another flesh of beasts, another of fishes, another of birds" (1 Corinthians 15:39).

didn't happen, and they come to that conclusion by only two ways that I can think of—either because the bible doesn't say it happened, or because they're too stuck up to believe that they came from monkeys, thus they ignore the evidence presented. But, what they don't realize (Christians mostly) is that evolution doesn't have to live outside of religion. By their reasoning, they should be saying that dinosaurs are a belief, because we only have bones, no actual evidence of their existence. The bible may not say it happened, but it also doesn't say it didn't. One of my two closest friends is a devout theist, and he believes in the bible, but he also believes in both the big bang and evolution.[15] He thinks that they are the tools god used to create. He thinks that they are the real-world reaction to the actions of god, the spiritual world connecting to the physical world and controlling it through physical means. Constantly speaking against something in the face of evidence without supplying evidence or even arguing to the contrary is called stubborn ignorance.

Evolution and god can exist side by side. Now who's the dreamer? Who's caught up in fantasy and ignoring the truth?

* * *

Ray, you wrote: << **Mother evolution would fix things up. Perhaps she could make another 'big bang' and the earth would expand. Or perhaps she would cause everyone to shrink in size ... she's done a good job so far in creating flowers, birds, fruits, trees, seasons, the incredible human body, etc. Nothing is too hard for God Evolution.** >>

I've just thought of a major flaw in the creationist argument. You say that because of things like "fruits, trees, seasons, the incredible human body," there has to be a creator, as it is unlikely that things like this came about on their own. Well, there is a huge gaping hole in this logic that I don't think anyone's caught yet. Take the human body for example. You say it is so complex that it couldn't have come about without a creator. Yet for your explanation, you say that something infinitely more complex created it, and that that infinitely complex being has no creator, nor did it evolve or come about by any means; it simply has been in existence forever.

This logic simply compounds the question by answering it with an even bigger question. Using the age-old watchmaker argument, that would be like saying that the watch was made by the watchmaker, but the watchmaker's just been there.[16] I know you will probably respond by telling me I should read your book, so if you

16 This is the age-old "Who made God?" question. Like space, God has no beginning and no end. We dwell in the dimension of "time," and because we are subject to it laws, logic demands that everything must have a beginning and an end. God dwells in "eternity," and He is therefore not subject to time. God flicks through time as we flick through the pages of a book. This is made clearly evident when one studies the incredible prophecies of the Bible. (See Matthew 24, Luke 21, 2 Timothy 3, etc.)

17 Mr. Franz was sent a copy of *God Doesn't Believe in Atheists,* which addresses the question, "Who made God?" He was also sent a Christmas present some time later. It is interesting to note that after reading this book, Mr. Ron Barrier (spokesperson for American Atheists, Inc.) withdrew his challenge to debate me. When this fact was made public, he reinstated the challenge. The debate may be freely heard on www.livingwaters.com/listen.shtml.

18 King James Version has been quoted in this publication. However, for the sake of readability, "hath" has been changed to "has" in a number of places.

19 Encouraging Christians put God to the test is not new. Two thousand years ago Jesus was given a similar challenge by the devil.(See Matthew 4:5-7.)

think I should read it, why don't you send me a copy, [17] or maybe even just a file of the book's text. I promise not to give the copy to anyone else without your permission first (being a writer I know the value of the copyright).

Unless you tell me otherwise, I am going to assume that you do not credit the bible as being completely true, nor is it the word of god, on the grounds that you turned down the test that I offered you. Please notify me if this is not true, why it is not true, and why you turned down the test, if you actually did turn down the test. If you accept my challenge, please let me know. I will wait a reasonable amount of time for your response before I post our correspondence to the Godless Zone message board.

Unless you tell me otherwise, I am going to assume that you do not credit the bible as being completely true, nor is it the word of god, on the grounds that you turned down the test that I offered you.

James, here is the reason I haven't answered you regarding the drinking of poison—(there is no nice way to put this other than to quote the wisdom of Solomon): "Answer not a fool according to his folly."[18] I don't have to prove anything to you. I would never be so foolish myself as to put God to the test.[19]

* * *

Also, what was your honest opinion of the flaw I pointed out in the creationist theory? I am going to bring up this point any time a theist wants to begin to "logically prove the existence of god," because the very foundation for god himself is completely illogical.

I am embarrassed to answer you—it's like trying to prove to a fish that there is an ocean.

Are you saying that you wouldn't be comfortable saying, "I believe there is a god?"

Of course—I would feel stupid. I believed in God before I was a Christian. Now I "know" Him. Big difference.

* * *

I'm talking about your version of god who would send someone to Hell just for not believing in him.

You are making me re-write my books. God will not send you to Hell for not believing in Him. You will go to Hell for lying, stealing, and committing adultery. In fact, God will not send you to Hell. A judge doesn't send a criminal to prison. His crimes send him there.

And, just to let you know, you may call me the fool, but the folly you speak of—this fool read it from the bible you hold so dear. The folly is yours, fool.

I didn't call you a fool. You read that into it.

Mark 16: 16-18—This is in Jesus' words: "He who believes and is baptized will be saved; but he who does not believe will be condemned."

Also, just wondering about your intent by saying, <<You're making me re-write my books.>> I took it in a positive light and saw it as a compliment, as you saying that I am providing insight into the questions of the unbelievers so that maybe you can make them more explicit to what people such as myself are asking.

You are making me go over the same old boring arguments I have gone over literally thousands of times before (no exaggeration).

This is the third time I've sent this to you, Ray: Mark 16: 16-18—This is in Jesus' words: "He who believes and is baptized will be saved; but he who does not believe will be condemned ... and if they drink anything deadly, it will by no means hurt them; they will lay hands on the sick, and they will recover."

Remember this from the *Test of Faith*? It says, "He who does NOT BELIEVE will be CONDEMNED." Read it this time, please.

* * *

No, actually it's not complex, as I am quite intelligent (Calculus and Physics were my favorite classes in high school, and Calculus was my best, finishing with 104%.) There's no semantics to be played; your analogy is very clear in its intent. But did you know that humans can literally make analogies explain anything, even if it's not true? That's why humans use analogies—because they're easy to understand, can be used in any argument, and are often convincing.

But, when they're the only thing you're arguing with, the "convincing" part begins to fall to pieces (Also, your analogy makes assumptions within the analogy, which is even worse.)

* * *

James. It may come as a shock to you, but there are many things I don't understand in the Bible. Mark Twain said, "It's not the things I don't understand in the Bible that bother me, but the things I do understand."[20] ... that God will punish liars, thieves, etc.

[20] Actual quote: "It ain't the parts of the Bible that I can't understand that bother me, it is the parts that I do understand." At the time, I presumed that Mark Twain was an atheist. He was certainly anti-Christian. However, I later discovered the following: Mark Twain's cynical nature is apparent in his earliest big success, *Innocents Abroad*. His attacks on hypocrisy and organized religion appealed to his readers and contributed greatly to his success. While his famous novels show playful disrespect toward clergy and worship, his lectures, essays and letters depict Twain unfurled ... with religion, government, and society besieged by his razor wit. Christianity, which attained new levels of pomposity during the Victorian era, vexed Twain to the extreme. "If Christ were here, there is one thing he would not be—a Christian," he says in his *Mark Twain's Notebook*. Despite his oft-quoted anti-Christian proclamations, Mark Twain was not an atheist. Throughout his life, he referred to God and man's immortal soul as extant. In *Mark Twain, A Biography*, Twain is quoted as saying, "I have never seen what to me seemed an atom of proof that there is a future life. And yet—I am inclined to expect one." He was able to separate his

criticisms from his somewhat limited spirituality throughout most of his adult life. In his later years, events caused him to harden. From www.wagg.com/Writings/mysterious.htm.

21 The atheist is the ultimate gambler. He is playing Russian roulette with a fully loaded gun. After he dies, he will stand before God in judgment, whether he believes in a Creator or not.

22 This isn't a reference to the good people of Alabama, but to the snake-handling churches in that state.

Mark Twain was an atheist, did you know that? That's why he said that quote. You should read this. It's Twain's "Letters to the Earth," and it was published after Twain's death by his request so that he wouldn't be persecuted for writing it.

<<Mark Twain was an atheist. >> **He won't be one now.**[21]

* * *

No, no no no no ... I know you won't take the test, that's not why I sent you that quote. I shouldn't have included the entire text of the message. Did you read the part below where I emphasized the point I was getting at? This is the third time I've sent this to you, Ray.

Here's my answer again for your "test": I would never handle snakes or deliberately drink poison. God gave me a brain and I will continue to use it. Again, if you are so excited about your test, take it to Alabama (they would love it).[22] I repeat, "I will never take your little test." What part of "never" don't you understand? Get it?

* * *

You asked: <<I don't know what you are referring to when you say you will go to Hell for not believing. I don't know of any Bible verse. Show me one.>>

16

I responded by sending this quote, which I at first included with the test of faith, but I am only pulling out the part I am using this time, and I'm capitalizing what I wish to emphasize: Mark 16:16-18—This is in Jesus' words:

"He who believes and is baptized will be saved; but HE WHO DOES NOT BELIEVE WILL BE CONDEMNED."

You will have to bear with me for the answer: A man, who trusts a parachute to save him, is saved from the consequences of breaking the law of gravity because he put on a parachute. (Please don't play semantics with my words, "breaking the law of gravity," etc.) A man, who refuses to trust in a parachute, doesn't perish because he refused it. He perishes primarily because he transgressed the law of gravity. Had he put it on, he would have been saved.

If you refuse to "believe" (trust)[23] in the Savior, you will perish, not because you didn't "believe," *but because you transgressed the Law of God.* Again, God won't punish you for not trusting in His mercy. He will punish you because you are a liar, a thief, and an adulterer at heart.

This is a little complex, and I'm no genius at expressing this, but it does make sense if you think it through.

[23] The Greek word used for "believe" in the New Testament is *pistos*, which means to "trust."

17

Many Christians don't understand this point and offend non-Christians with their thoughtless, "You will go to Hell if you don't believe in Jesus."

<< No, actually it's not complex, as I am quite intelligent. (Calculus and Physics were my favorite classes in high school, and Calculus was my best, finishing with 104%.) >>

24 This sounds a little rude, but it wasn't meant to be. It's the truth. I have found that many professing intellectuals lack any semblance of wisdom or common sense.

Not impressed.[24]

I wasn't trying to IMPRESS you. I was just letting you know that I have the mental capacity to understand complexity and method, but I was mostly just making small talk. Thanks for being friendly.

BTW: Who do you thank for your blessings?

I'm not talking about me … I'm talking about this (this makes the fifth time): Mark 16:16-18—This is in Jesus' words: "He who believes and is baptized will be saved; but he who does not believe will be condemned." If I had been talking about myself, I wouldn't have said, "Still, no matter what it is, to 'punish' SOMEONE for not believing you exist is selfish."

I don't know how many times I have to tell you—God will not punish you for not believing in Him. He will

punish you for lying, stealing, etc., of which you have admitted guilt.

Yes, and it's god's law that all must believe in him or perish. To break that law is to break the law of god and suffer the consequences. That's all I wanted to know—that god would punish someone (not me specifically, mind you) JUST for not believing in him, and that is, in mine and most people's opinion, selfish, cruel, and unjust. If someone hurt my feelings, whether I created them or not, I would hope to be damned to put them through pain even remotely close to what Christians say god would put me through. It's just a scare tactic, a principal piece of what's called, "propaganda."

"HE WHO DOES NOT BELIEVE WILL BE CONDEMNED."

I repeat. If you don't trust in a parachute, you will suffer the consequences for breaking the law of gravity. You perish primarily because you break the law, not because you didn't trust the 'chute.

Still, no matter what it is, to "punish" SOMEONE for not believing you exist is selfish.

I give up trying to explain this to you.

* * *

Humans are very creative and intelligent ...

I don't believe that. We can't make one grain of sand from nothing. Some even deny they were created. Some believe they come from monkeys. I'm embarrassed by that.

Well, I hope the millions of creative people down the years who have contributed to the existence of the computer and Internet you're currently using know how much you appreciate them.

Any abilities we have are God-given.

* * *

I was just wondering if you had ANY points that you wanted to bring up that would actually make this a debate, or answer ANY of the facts which blatantly support evolution, which is where this debate started in the first place. If you don't, this is what happens (in debates):

You cannot account otherwise for these occurrences (see my 1st email), or else you know nothing about evolution. In either case, you have no way to intelligently deny the evolutionary process, which totally negates any argumentation that you gave on your web page (none of which was even close to convincing). You have given no valid arguments, and therefore if you cannot bring up any counter evidence, additional possible explanations for the facts, or ways to point out how my inferences were specifically arrived at wrong. You must accept now that you have no place disputing evolution and the debate will be over, Sir. Bring up a counter argument (which is substantiated by FACTS) or lose and accept defeat. That's the way it goes. (Did you ever take debate in school? I did.) Accept that you cannot deny evolution, or else prove why you can now. That's all there is to it.

* * *

Good, because you've just been telling me the same thing over and over while ignoring my point. I know you say I won't be punished just for not believing, but also for my other "sins," but your bible says that someone who does not believe will be condemned; it does not say, "He who does not believe and commits other sins will be condemned." That means if I knew someone whose only sin was not believing, they would be going to hell along with me and Jeffrey Dahmer,[25] all three of us to suffer the same fate.[26] Justice? I think not. If you don't get my point this time, I'm going to give up trying to explain it to YOU.

[Mr. Franz then stopped corresponding for two months.]

25 Jeffrey Lionel Dahmer was an American serial killer who murdered 17 men between 1978 and 1991. Most of his victims were African American men whom he subjected to sexual assaults. He achieved notoriety after his arrest following the discovery of several decaying bodies in acid vats in his apartment. Severed heads were found in his refrigerator and an altar of candles and human skulls was found in his closet. Accusations soon surfaced that he had practiced necrophilia and cannibalism. He admitted to eating the biceps of his eighth victim, Ernest Miller, whose skeleton he also kept.

26 "Sinners often accuse God of being unjust, because they assume that everyone will receive the same punishment in hell. God's judgment, however, will be according to righteousness" (Acts 17:31). This verse (Matthew 11:24) shows that there will be *degrees* of punishment. (See also Mark 6:11.) (From *The Evidence Bible* Bridge-Logos Publishers.)

27 This is reference to: "Charles Dawson, a British lawyer and amateur geologist, who announced in 1912 his discovery of pieces of a human skull and an apelike jaw in a gravel pit near the town of Piltdown, England. Dawson's announcement stopped the scorn cold. Experts instantly declared Piltdown Man (estimated to be 300,000 to one million years old), the evolutionary find of the century. Darwin's missing link had been identified.

"Or so it seemed for the next 40 or so years. Then, in the early fifties ... scientists began to suspect misattribution. In 1953 that suspicion gave way to a full-blown scandal: Piltdown Man was a hoax. Radiocarbon tests proved that its skull belonged to a 600-year-old woman, and its jaw to a 500-year-old orangutan from the East Indies." *Our Times—the Illustrated History of the 20th Century* (Turner Publishing, 1995, page 94).

The Piltdown Man fraud wasn't an isolated incident. The famed "Nebraska Man" was built from one tooth, which was later found to be that of an extinct pig. "Java Man" was found in the early 20th Century and was nothing more than a piece of skull, a fragment of a thighbone and three molar teeth. The rest came from the deeply fertile imaginations of

* * *

Hey, it's been a while since we've talked, but I don't wish to start any debates with you this time, I just wanted to ask you an honest question which humbly begs for an honest answer. Now, read this question closely, as it is very carefully worded, and asks for a very specific answer, which I feel is the best way to ask complex questions. Being a devoted creationist, I felt it would be best to address this question to you, as you have a well-respected opinion in the Christian world. Well, enough with the small talk, let me just get right to it.

On the subject of evolution, I simply wanted to know specifically which processes of evolution or modern evidences either do not convince you that it's true, or prove to you that it's false. Now, I am asking for specific processes or modern evidences, such as the ones I offered to you way back when we first talked. Also, pertaining to the basic overall idea of evolution, what about it specifically does not hold water in your opinion? You must, of course, exclude in your answer any processes or evidences which have proven to be false or hoaxes.[27]

Looking forward to hearing from you,
James D. Franz

James, I hope you are well. I have never been convinced that there is any concrete evidence for the theory.[28] None. Zilch. Zip. It's all faith. Best wishes, Ray

And I hope you are well also. Oh, and thank you for the books. I am enjoying them greatly. The two extras you threw in were quite a treat.

But, your answer does not exactly address the question, and if you simply do not wish to answer it I understand. Also, if you do not have the time to right now, I can wait as long as you need if you want to type out a detailed answer. The answer I want though is an at least somewhat detailed description of some of the processes or evidences of evolution that exist and support evolution, and other alternative explanations you may have to attribute the evidence to other phenomena. Also, if you could explain why the processes that make up evolution are either improbable or impossible. If you could also address evolution as a whole and why you believe it to be wrong and what about the idea makes you think that, I would be very thankful. I hope you don't mind my "poking," but I'm trying to gather more information on the creationist view of evolution and what other ideas are existent in this world about our origins. Thank you very much for your time. Peace, James D. Franz

plaster of Paris workers. "Heidelberg Man" came from a jawbone, a large chin section, and a few teeth. Most scientists reject the jawbone because it's similar to that of modern man. It was also discovered that "Neanderthal Man" had a skull that belonged to a human, not an ape.

28 Before I was a Christian I believed in the theory, but that wasn't based on any evidence. It was blind faith that what I occasionally saw on television about the issue was indeed true.

29 All humanity is spiritually blind: "But if our gospel be hid, it is hid to them that are lost: In whom the god of this world has blinded the minds of them which believe not, lest the light of the glorious gospel of Christ, who is the image of God, should shine unto them" (II Corinthians 4:3-4). "Having the understanding darkened, being alienated from the life of God through the ignorance that is in them, because of the blindness of their heart" (Ephesians 4:18).

30 This is rather strange— to see James give a capital letter for "Almighty." He goes to great pains in every letter to make sure God is not given a capital letter.

31 "The wicked, through the pride of his countenance,

will not seek after God: God is not in all his thoughts. His ways are always grievous; thy judgments are far above out of his sight: as for all his enemies, he puffs at them … He has said in his heart, God has forgotten: he hides his face; he will never see it" (Psalm 10:44-5, 10).

32 Dr. Kent Hovind, an authority on evolution has had a long-standing offer. He will give $250,000 "to anyone who can offer any scientific proof for evolution." You can find Dr. Hovind's offer at: www.drdino.com/ articles.php?spec=67 Evolution *cannot* be proven. It is something accepted by "faith."

33 Evolution and "religion" may be compatible (Pope John Paul embraced the theory of evolution as gospel truth for Roman Catholics). However, the theory and the Scriptures are diametrically opposed to one another.

34 It is the professing atheist who is (willfully) blind to the genius of God's creative hand. Bertrand Russell was on his deathbed when a friend asked him, "You've been the world's most famous atheist most of your life, and now you're going o die. What if you were wrong? What would you say to God if you met Him?

I am being asked by a man who was born in darkness to give my thoughts on "evidence" that light doesn't exist.

How about I start making totally insipid assumptions about you too, huh? Okay, first of all I wasn't "born into darkness,"[29] I was born and raised as a theist, a strong believer in the Almighty,[30] and I was very happy there. But since, I have grown to learn that I must put away the things of childhood, and I have learned that though god is a good thing to look to, it does not necessarily exist. Since then, I've been even happier, because I now know that I am in control of my life and my destiny, and I don't have to fear eternal damnation for every little transgression.[31] Also, I'm not asking you for evidence that the "light," as I take it you mean god, doesn't exist. I'm asking you for the information you have on evolution, a strong scientific[32] theory with many interesting outlines as to its details. As I said before, the evolution and religion do not go against each other.[33] It's religion's inherent ignorance of reality which blinds people.[34] For instance, do you speak against evolution because other christians speak out against it, or do you speak out against evolution because you have looked into it, studied the evidences and process and concluded that it's just not likely? Don't respond to this question—I don't want you to answer me, I want you to answer yourself. I don't care, personally.

When it comes to the question of the reality of god, there are a few truths, and let me show you these:

Are there any arguments for god?

No.[35]

Does this mean god does not exist?

No.

Are there any arguments against god?

No.

Does this mean that god does exist?

No.

Is it likely that evolution happened?

Very.[36]

Is there evidence to support it? Yes.

Does this mean that god does not exist?

No.

Is it likely that the big bang happened?

Fairly.

Don't you think it's prudent at least to raise that question now, before it's too late?" The atheist replied: "I think I should say to Him: Sir, it appears that my atheistic hypothesis was erroneous. Would you mind answering me one wee little question? Why didn't you give us more evidence?" In the light of the glorious creation—flowers, birds, trees, the sun, the moon and the stars, only a blind man would ask such a question.

35 The greatest proof that a builder existed (even though he may not be seen or even known) is the building he made. *Every* building has a builder. One could not want better proof that there was a builder than to have the building as evidence. This simple principle can also be used with paintings and painters. Absolute proof that a painter existed is the painting. His existence is axiomatic. This is why the Bible says: "For the wrath of God is revealed from heaven against all ungodliness and unrighteousness of men, who hold the truth in unrighteousness; because that which may be known of God is manifest in them; for God has shown it unto them. For the invisible things of him from the creation of the world are clearly seen, being understood by the things that are made, even his eternal power and Godhead; so that they are without excuse: because that, when they knew God, they glorified him not as God, neither were thankful; but became vain in their imaginations, and their foolish heart was darkened. Professing themselves to be wise, they became fools ..." (Romans 1:18-22).

36 Evolution should not be taught. Dr. Colin Patterson, senior paleontologist, British Museum of Natural History, gave a keynote address at the American Museum of Natural History, New York City, in 1981. In it, he explained his sudden "anti-evolutionary" view: "One morning I woke up and ... it struck me that I had been working on this stuff for twenty years, and there was not one thing I knew about it. That's quite a shock to learn that one can be misled so long. ... I've tried putting a simple question to various people: 'Can you tell me anything you know about evolution, any one thing, any one thing that is true?' I tried that question on the geology staff at the Field Museum of Natural History and the only answer I got was silence. I tried it on the members of the Evolutionary Morphology Seminar in the University of Chicago, a very prestigious body of

Is there evidence to support it?

Yes.

Does this mean that god does not exist?

No.

Is there any evidence for creationism?

No.

Does this mean it didn't happen?

No.

Look, Ray, I don't speak out for evolution because I am an atheist. I studied and agreed with evolution long before I became an unbeliever. I believed in evolution while I believed in god,[37] and saw no disagreement between the two.[38] I'm not talking religion when I ask you about evolution, I'm talking science fact.[39] Apparently you think I'm starting another religious debate with you, but I'm just asking for you to show me what grounds you stand on to discount a scientific theory.[40] If you're so ignorant as to deny the possibility of that which you have no knowledge, then I have no reason to be talking with you. This has been a perfectly good waste of my time, but at least it has provided me with insight as to the mind of the "ignorant christian."

Good day. I will speak with you no more on subjects which baffle you.

No argument. Sin gives pleasure ... for a season.[41] You still have to face God on Judgment Day.

You call me sinful, you call my beliefs wrong, you call my heart evil. I call you ignorant. Who's right? Who's wrong? Is anybody right? Is anybody wrong?

James. God's right. We're wrong. See John 8:31, 32.[42] Better repent and trust Jesus today. Treat every day as though it is your last ... one day you'll be right.

I'm off to New Zealand for a week. Leaving tonight. God bless, Ray

Oh, man—I am really jealous. New Zealand is absolutely gorgeous country—I plan to visit there sometime, as well as Australia! Have a nice time, and hey if you take any pictures be sure to post them on your website! I'm sure everyone would love to see what a beautiful place it is up there.

As for being right and wrong, the questions still stand. If god exists, he's right because he defines right and wrong, but does that mean it's outside of our rights to question him? God should want to learn from his creation. If he does not, then I do not wish to

evolutionists, and all I got there was silence for a long time and eventually one person said, 'I do know one thing—it ought not to be taught in high school.'" (From *The Evidence Bible*).

37 Evolutionist *Stephen Hawking* wrote, "It would be very difficult to explain why the universe should have begun in just this way, except as the act of a God who intended to create beings like us" *(A Brief History of Time).* He also stated: "Then we shall ... be able to take part in the discussion of the question of why it is that we and the universe exist. If we find the answer to that, it would be the ultimate triumph of human reason—for then we would know the mind of God."

38 Fossil evidence points to creation. "The creation account in Genesis and the theory of evolution could not be reconciled. One must be right and the other wrong. The story of the fossils agrees with the account of Genesis. In the oldest rocks we did not find a series of fossils covering the gradual changes from the most primitive creatures to developed forms but rather, in the oldest rocks, developed species suddenly appeared. Between every species there was a complete absence of intermediate fossils." – *D. B. Gower* (biochemist), "Scientist Rejects Evolution," *Kentish Times.*

39 Evolution—the origin of sexes. Almost all forms of complex life have both male and female—horses, dogs, humans, moths, monkeys, fish, elephants, birds, etc. The male needs the female to reproduce, and the female needs the male to reproduce. *One cannot carry on life without the other.* Which then came first according to the evolutionary theory? If a male came into being before a female, how did the male of each species reproduce *without* females? How is it possible that a male and a female each spontaneously came into being, yet they have complex, complementary reproductive systems If each sex was able to reproduce without the other, why (and how) would they have developed a reproductive system that requires both sexes in order for the species to survive?

"I myself am convinced that the theory of evolution, especially the extent to which it has been applied, will be one of the great jokes in the history books of the future. Posterity will marvel that so flimsy and dubious an hypothesis could be accepted with the incredible credulity that it has." *Malcolm Muggeridge,* British journalist and

follow him. Any benefit should benefit him as well. I've read your bible verses, and I'd like to share with you some wise words that I'm sure everyone has told someone else: Don't believe everything you read. What makes the bible right? Because it says it's right. What does that prove? I'll tell you what that proves, it proves that the writers of the bible knew that people would doubt it. The truth needs no defending, so why does the bible defend itself so even within its own pages? But, I fear you will never listen.

Oh well, and do have a good time in New Zealand.

"God should want to learn from his creation!"

You have just confirmed that you are (as I once was) blind. God is omniscient. That means He knows everything.[43] You can't teach Him anything.

If god is all-knowing, then he cannot make choices. If god is all-knowing, then he knew his creations would be imperfect. If god is all-knowing, he already knows if I'm going to heaven or hell and there's nothing he or I can do about it. If god is all-knowing, he would already know all outcomes and thus not have any control over them. If god was all-knowing, he would have known long before that Eve would have eaten the apple.[44] If god is all-knowing, then he has no right to punish for things even HE cannot change. If god is all-knowing, then there would be no point at all to his creation.

If god is all-knowing, he already knows if I'm going to heaven or hell and there's nothing he or I can do about it.

That won't hold water on Judgment Day. You will have eternity to regret such silly attempts to justify rebellion.

* * *

I never heard back from you, so I was wondering if you got this and the second email I sent you after you left for New Zealand. Did you enjoy yourself? I hope so. I just got back on Sunday from Oregon, and what a beautiful state that is! If only it didn't rain so much, but that's that.

Of course, I've seen pictures and I know that New Zealand is quite a bit more beautiful than Oregon.

Well, just below is a response I sent to you, and I think it's a really good one, so I decided to make sure you got it and I forwarded it to you.

Hope you are well, James D. Franz

philosopher (From *The Evidence Bible*.)

40 God made them male and female. If every creature "evolved" with no Creator, there are numerous problems. Take for instance the first bird. Was it male or female? Let's say it was a male. How did it produce offspring without a mate? If a female evolved, why did it evolve with differing reproductive organs? Did it evolve by chance, or did it evolve because it knew that it was needed by the male of the species? How did it know what needed to be evolved if its brain hadn't yet evolved? Did the bird breathe? Did it breathe before it evolved lungs? How did it do this? Why did it evolve lungs if it was happily surviving without them? Did the bird have a mouth? How did it eat before it had evolved a mouth? Where did the mouth send the food before a stomach evolved? How did the bird have energy if it didn't eat (because it didn't yet have a mouth)? How did the bird see what there was to eat before its eyes evolved? Evolution is intellectual suicide. It is an embarrassment. "Evolution is a fairy tale for grown-ups. This theory has helped nothing in the progress of science. It is useless." Professor Louis Bounoure, Director of Research, National Center of Scientific Research. "Scientists who go about teaching that evolution is a fact of life are great con-men, and the story they are telling may be the greatest hoax ever. In explaining evolution, we do not have one iota of fact." Dr. T. N. Tahmisian, Atomic Energy Commission (From *The Evidence Bible*).

41 "By faith Moses, when he was come to years, refused to be called the son of Pharaoh's daughter; choosing rather to suffer affliction with the people of God than to enjoy the pleasures of sin for a season" (Hebrews 11:24). "Why does the way of the wicked prosper? Why are those happy who deal so treacherously?" (Jeremiah 12:1).

42 "Then said Jesus to those Jews which believed on him, If you continue in my word, then are you my disciples indeed; And you shall know the truth, and the truth shall make you free" (John 8:31-32).

43 "Neither is there any creature that is not manifest in his sight: but all things are naked and opened unto the eyes of him with whom we have to do" (Hebrew 4:13). "O Lord, you have searched me, and known me. You know my downsitting and my uprising, you understand my thought

You are really convinced that you've got all the answers. You've really got yourself tricked into believing that you're 100% right. Well, let me tell you just one thing. Do you consider yourself to be compassionate of other humans? If you're right, as you say you are, and you believe that, then how can you sleep at night? When you speak with me, you are speaking with someone who you believe is walking directly into eternal damnation, into an endless onslaught of horrendous pain which your "loving" god created, yet you stand by and do nothing. If you believed one bit that thousands every day were falling into an eternal and unchangeable fate, you should be running the streets mad with rage at their blindness. That's equivalent to standing on a street corner and watching every person that passes you walk blindly directly into the path of a bus and die, yet you stand idly by and do nothing. You're just twiddling your thumbs, happy in the knowledge that one day that "walk" signal will shine your way across the road. Think about it, Ray. Imagine the horrors hell must have in store if the bible is true. You're just going to allow that to happen and not care about saving anyone but yourself? If you're right, then you're an uncaring, unemotional and purely selfish [expletive] that has no right to talk about subjects such as love and caring.

James, you're right. Absolutely right. If it is true that God is a God of Justice and that He will punish all sin, every Christian should be doing what you say. You are right—we shouldn't sleep at night. Actually, I don't. I get up most nights around midnight to pray for people like you. Have done so for 14 years. I am horrified at even one person going to Hell. I do "run around the streets mad with rage at their blindness," but if I betray how concerned I am for people, I would probably be locked up in an insane asylum. I take a team to Santa Monica every Friday night and preach in the open air until I'm exhausted, speaking to people like you … I have a license to do so. I go out every Tuesday and Friday and plead with people to consider the claims of the Gospel. So I'm not twiddling my thumbs, and I'm not happy. You see, I don't "believe" there is a Hell. I know so. Remember that.[45]

I hope you don't mind, but I'm going to quote your letter when I speak in churches. Most Christians are guilty of what you say.[46] A great preacher said the same thing. Charles Spurgeon said, "We need to be ashamed at the mere suspicion of unconcern."

Thank you for being bold enough to say what you did. God bless, Ray

afar off. You compass my path and my lying down, and are acquainted with all my ways. For there is not a word in my tongue, but, lo, O Lord, you know it altogether. You have beset me behind and before, and laid your hand upon me. Such knowledge is too wonderful for me; it is high, I cannot attain unto it. Whither shall I go from your spirit? or whither shall I flee from your presence? If I ascend up into heaven, you are there: if I make my bed in hell, behold, you are there. If I take the wings of the morning, and dwell in the uttermost parts of the sea; Even there shall your hand lead me, and your right hand shall hold me. If I say, Surely the darkness shall cover me; even the night shall be light about me. Yea, the darkness hides not from you; but the night shines as the day: the darkness and the light are both alike to you" (Psalm 139:1-12).

44 The Bible makes no mention of an "apple." Eve ate the fruit of the Tree of the Knowledge of Good and Evil. (See Genesis 3:5.)

45 There are a number of reasons that the existence of Hell is more than mere belief. First. There is the fact that the Bible makes many references to a literal Hell. If it wasn't filled with scientific facts and medical facts written thousands of years before man discovered them, and prophecies that have been and are being fulfilled to every jot and title, one could dismiss it as merely the writing of man. However, these things are stark evidence that this is no ordinary Book, but it is indeed the Word of God. Second. One has merely to think a little for Hell to be reasonable. In the face of creation, only a fool denies that there is a Creator [see Psalm 14:1-2], and no one (in his right mind) would believe that God is morally bad. Obviously there's a Creator, and obviously God is good by nature. Think now of the 100,000 murderers that were never brought to justice during the 1990s (homicide in the U.S. has a 50 percent success rate, and during that decade there were approximately 200,000 murders). Think of how we (even as sinful human beings) spend millions of dollars just to bring one murderer to justice. How much more then will Almighty God see to it that each one of those murderers receives justice? He cannot turn a blind eye to one who takes the life of another human being. If a human judge did that, he would be evil, and should therefore be brought to justice himself. So, when a human judge has a guilty murderer standing before him, the judge, if he is a good man,

I would be very happy to have that quoted. For me, personally, it's a message that I give christians telling them that I understand why they act toward me the way they do. I understand that the reason they would ever begin preaching to me is out of care and concern. I'm also glad that the idea of hell makes you uncomfortable. There are times when I struggle a little with my idea of what comes after death, taking discomfort in it, [47] but I know that the day cannot be avoided or put off. But, just let me offer you one piece of advice, and I'd like you to listen to it and consider it very deeply. I'm going to walk right now with the assumption that there is a god, alright? I'm backtracking to when I believed. Now, there are two large things you have to consider when it comes to the idea of hell. First of all, what has ever proven that the bible was not tainted a bit by the hand of man when it was written?[48] What shows that it is pure, besides it's saying that it is? Second, if god is one bit loving, do you think he would allow such a thing to consume his creation? Would you allow your children to go to hell if you could stop it? Do you consider the idea horrendous?

Would you allow hell to exist? If you would not allow hell to exist, and you are just a human, imagine for one moment how an all-loving GOD would see hell, and keep in mind that he can do away with it and Satan at any moment.

Also, if god is perfect, he perfectly understands the idea of justice. What kind of justice is eternal torment? What purpose does it serve?

The main point here is: What is justice when behavior is not corrected?

It is, in this sense, sadistic torture. That's it. Even if there is a hell, it cannot be eternal and be a form of justice at the same time. You need to consider these things, Ray. You've been taking the bible for granted too long.[49] Do you think it's possible that some of the ideas in it are the fabrication of man, with the positive intent of tailoring society for the better?

Realize here that I'm not trying one bit to undermine or doubt your belief in god. All I'm asking is that you look at things from god's shoes for a moment. If hell is justice, then it cannot be eternal. If hell is eternal, then god is cruel. If god is cruel, then all should be wary of his wrath, yourself included. There is a lot about the bible that does not make sense.

More christians need to consider these things instead of blindly following a book that is thousands of years old.

can't just let him go. He must ensure that the guilty man is punished. If God is good, He must (by nature) punish the murderer. But He is so good, he is also going to punish rapists, thieves, liars, adulterers, fornicators, and those who have lived in rebellion against the inner light that God has given to every man. The place of God's punishment is called, "Hell." C.S. Lewis said, "There is no doctrine which I would more willingly remove from Christianity than the doctrine of hell, if it lay in my power. But it has the full support of Scripture and, especially, of our Lord's own words; it has always been held by the Christian Church, and it has the support of reason."

46 A survey in *Christianity Today* found that only 1 percent of their readership had witnessed to somebody "recently."

47 Pride will often cause a man to say that the thought of death gives him "discomfort." In truth, the fear of death holds him in what the Scriptures refer to as "bondage": "Forasmuch then as the children are partakers of flesh and blood, he also himself likewise took part of the same; that through death he might destroy him that had the power of death, that is, the devil; And deliver them who through fear of death were all their lifetime subject to bondage" (Hebrew 2:14-15).

48 To this point in my life, I have been reading the Bible every day (without fail) for 33 years, and I have never found a mistake. I have found many seeming contradictions, and what I perceived as a "mistake," but upon investigation I found that it was *my* mistake. It must have been a test for those folk who believed the Bible when it said the earth was round [see Isaiah 40:22] and freely floated in space (Job 26:7), when science at that time and logic common logic adamantly maintained otherwise.

49 Faith in the Bible as the revelation of the Creator isn't taken in blind faith. There is evidence of the fingerprint of God for those who are open to reason. Take, for example the the many scientific facts in the Bible, all of which were written thousands of years before man discovered them. (See Appendix.)

50 "For the preaching of the cross is to them that perish foolishness; but unto us which are saved it is the power of God." "But unto them which are called, both Jews and Greeks, Christ the power of God, and the wisdom of God." "That your faith should not stand in the

Please let me know your thoughts on this, I would love to hear some feedback. And please, do consider it with an open and thinking mind. Oh, and anything I said in my last email was not directed toward you personally. Peace, James D. Franz

James. Two things. First: I wasn't converted by the Bible. I was transformed by the power of God[50] on the 25th of April, 1972. It was so radical, I am still reeling 27 years later. There hasn't been one (awakened) hour in all those years in which I was not conscious of God being with me. For the 22 years before my conversion, I didn't give God one moment's serious thought (no exaggeration). When I picked up a Bible after my conversion, it told me what had happened to me (I had no idea). If I had read the Bible in an unconverted state, it wouldn't have made any sense to me. [51]

Second. Eternal punishment. If you read in the paper that a criminal received a $2 fine, you may presume that he committed a petty crime. However, if you read of man being given seven (multiple) life sentences, you may presume that his crime was heinous. The punishment given out gives you an idea of the seriousness of the crime. Eternal punishment gives us an idea of how seriously God views sin. Jesus said that if your eye causes you to sin, pluck it out, and cast it from you, [52] giving us an idea of how serious sin is. God warns that He sees sin as so heinous that He will damn sinners from life, love, laughter, and the wonderful creation He so lavished upon us ... forever. No reprieve. One strike and you are out. That makes me shudder. It so concerns me that I pleaded with non-Christians in "Speaker's Corner" almost every day for 12 years (in New Zealand). Each Friday night (as I have mentioned), I drive 60 miles and do the same thing in Santa Monica.

Also, God's judgment will be "according to righteousness." [53] That means everyone will get what they deserve. There will be no injustice on Judgment Day. [54] The Apostle Paul had a similar dilemma to your thoughts (in the Book of Romans). He brings out the thought that the fact of death spreading on all humanity just because of the sin of one man (Adam) may seem unfair. But then he brings out the "unfairness" that God gives the gift of everlasting life to undeserving sinners,[55] if they will obey Him. He says that the latter far outweighs the former.

If I find that I am sinking in quicksand, I would rather have someone pull me out first. Then, once I am safe, I can think about how I got in there, why this Stranger pulled me out, whether or not it was fair of Him to do so, etc.

wisdom of men, but in the power of God" (I Corinthians 1:18, 24, 2:5)

51 "But the natural man receives not the things of the Spirit of God: for they are foolishness unto him: neither can he know them, because they are spiritually discerned" (I Corinthians 2:14).

52 "And if your right eye offend you, pluck it out, and cast it from you: for it is profitable for you that one of your members should perish, and not that your whole body should be cast into hell. And if your right hand offend you, cut it off, and cast it from you: for it is profitable for you that one of your members should perish, and not that your whole body should be cast into hell" (Matthew 5:29-30).

53 "And he shall judge the world in righteousness, he shall minister judgment to the people in uprightness" (Psalm 9:8).

54 There will not be a "blanket" judgment for all of humanity. Notice that Jesus warns that hypocrites will receive a "greater" damnation: "And he said unto them in his doctrine, Beware of the scribes, which love to go in long clothing, and love salutations in the market-places, And the chief seats in the synagogues, and the uppermost rooms at feasts:

Which devour widows' houses, and for a pretence make long prayers: these shall receive greater damnation" (Mark 12:38-40).

55 "But not as the offence, so also is the free gift. For if through the offence of one many be dead, much more the grace of God, and the gift by grace, which is by one man, Jesus Christ, has abounded unto many. And not as it was by one that sinned, so is the gift: for the judgment was by one to condemnation, but the free gift is of many offences unto justification. For if by one man's offence death reigned by one; much more they which receive abundance of grace and of the gift of righteousness shall reign in life by one, Jesus Christ. Therefore as by the offence of one judgment came upon all men to condemnation; even so by the righteousness of one the free gift came upon all men unto justification of life. For as by one man's disobedience many were made sinners, so by the obedience of one shall many be made righteous" (Romans 5:15-19).

56 This is a wrong understanding of the purpose of justice. When a man rapes 3-4 teenage girls, then slits their throats, he is put to death not to have his "behavior

James, it is good to know you are well. God bless, Ray Comfort

Well, I enjoyed reading your response, but there was one part of my question that I'd still like to read your opinion on specifically. This is my opinion on hell here: "If god is one bit loving, do you think he would allow such a thing to consume his creation? Would YOU allow your children to go to hell if you COULD STOP it? Do you consider the idea horrendous? Would you allow hell to exist? If you would not allow hell to exist, and you find the idea disturbing, and keep in mind you are just a human, imagine for one moment how an all-loving GOD would see hell, and also keep in mind that he can do away with it and Satan at any moment. Also, if god is perfect, he perfectly understands the idea of justice. What kind of justice is eternal torment? What purpose does it serve?

The main point here is: What is justice when behavior is not corrected?[56] It is, in this sense, sadistic torture. That's it. Even if there is a hell, it cannot be eternal and be a form of justice at the same time.

One thing I've noticed about biblical christianity is that god seems to be playing a game, like this huge game of chess between himself and satan, with us as the pawns. There's no other possibility, or else god would not have allowed satan to exist. If the bible is true, then god has allowed satan to devastate his creation, misguide his children, but fights against him. That comes to two possibilities: either god is not powerful enough to destroy satan, which would go against much of the bible, or god allows him to exist for whatever grotesque reasons or games he has in mind. Do you have any ideas on this?

One of the big questions I have about this is, and you can just tell me your opinion on it if there is no scripture pertaining to it, why does god allow satan to act against his creation? Is it a game? Lack of power? An experiment or test? Tell me what you think. Sincerely, James D. Franz

"Would YOU allow your children to go to hell if you COULD STOP it?"

1. The analogy doesn't fit. We are not God's children. The Bible says Satan is our father.[57] It teaches that we are the enemy of God until we come to Jesus Christ.[58] His wrath abides on us. He hates the workers of iniquity.[59]

2. God is not "all loving." I don't know where you heard that. I've never said it. Neither does the Bible.[60]

3. Here's a murderer's dilemma: "I don't understand how a judge could send someone to prison for life for corrected," but that justice might be done.

57 "Wherein in time past you walked according to the course of this world, according to the prince of the power of the air, the spirit that now works in the children of disobedience: Among whom also we all had our conversation in times past in the lusts of our flesh, fulfilling the desires of the flesh and of the mind; and were by nature the children of wrath, even as others" (Ephesians 2:2-3). "You are of your father the devil, and the lusts of your father you will do. He was a murderer from the beginning, and abode not in the truth, because there is no truth in him. When he speaks a lie, he speaks of his own: for he is a liar, and the father of it" (John 8:44).

58 "You adulterers and adulteresses, know ye not that the friendship of the world is enmity with God? whosoever therefore will be a friend of the world is the enemy of God" (James 4:4). "For if, when we were enemies, we were reconciled to God by the death of his Son, much more, being reconciled, we shall be saved by his life" (Romans 5:10).

59 "The Lord tries the righteous: but the wicked and him that loves violence his soul hates" (Psalm 11:5).

60 The Bible teaches that God is also just, holy and righteous. To say that God is "all-loving" and not make reference to His other attributes is to create an idol.

61 I do understand the fact that Lucifer was cast to the earth.

mere murder of a few people … with no parole. It serves no purpose. It doesn't correct behavior. If he was a good man, he would forget about justice. I don't like him at all. He's sadistic."

4. I don't have any idea why Satan is around.[61]

Thanks for your response. It was quite different from what the usual humdrum I hear from christians. I've written quite a response here, and I hope you don't mind the way I talk on and on, but I've got a lot of questions about this matter and you've been more helpful to me than most christians who simply shrug off the questions and view them as insulting. I hope you don't see them as insulting as well, and if you do, I apologize. But, here I've got a big outline filled with a lot of questions that go from your four points you addressed. Please read through these, as they really beg a detailed answer, but mostly I'd really just like to hear your opinions on these matters. Take your time—I can wait a month if it takes a month—that old "Better late than never" adage.

As for your answers:

1) Interesting point. Here's another idea: every evil thing that is tainting god's creation, he allowed entrance. Why? Think of Genesis, Adam and Eve

in Eden. God placed the tree of knowledge there and told Adam not to eat of its fruit (but apparently had the foresight to guard the tree of life). Of course, we all know that Eve ate from the tree, and then Adam did too, after the serpent coaxed them into it. So now, how did god allow this? First of all, he created the serpent that did this—and don't try to make this serpent out to be Satan, the Bible makes it very clear that this was just a serpent[62]—he created a creature with an apparently instinctual desire to taint his two people he just made. Also, he puts them in a garden, with a tree they're not supposed to eat as well as something which he knows (unless he is not omniscient, which you yourself have said of him) will get them to eat the fruit, and lets them go about their business. Just as well, he also created both of these people with innate curiosity which he also created!

It's kind of like setting a gun between two children just to see if one gets shot.

There are a few possibilities. First, god was conducting an experiment, to see if they would eat the fruit, which would not be possible if god was omniscient, as he would already know the outcome. Also, having created this man and woman, he created their every desire and feeling, including what drove them to eat the fruit, and also the snake which tempted them

62 "But I fear, lest by any means, as the serpent beguiled Eve through his subtlety, so your minds should be corrupted from the simplicity that is in Christ" (II Corinthians 11:3). "And the great dragon was cast out, that old serpent, called the Devil, and Satan, which deceives the whole world: he was cast out into the earth, and his angels were cast out with him" (Revelation 12:9).

and he created the snake's desire to temp them!!! Now, if god did not know what would happen, he's not omniscient. If god created them, but didn't know the feelings he created within them, then he's not omnipotent. Only if he has limitations to his power and knowledge could this possibly be a test. Which would you say? Now, if he is omnipotent and omniscient, then this has to all be a game. Of course, if I had existed forever, I bet I'd be bored too. I'd want to create an equal to battle with, but I wouldn't create beings with feelings and emotions who will just become the unfortunate and endlessly suffering casualties of the game.

What do you think of all this?

2) As for the "All loving," I guess I just got that from years of doe-eyed, dreamy christians who made god out to be whatever they wanted. Thanks for letting me know there is no biblical backing for this statement.

3) Okay, first of all the American justice system is not in any way equal to god's justice—I have enough distaste for the American way altogether that I want to move to another country as soon as I can afford it—and I MEAN that! If god was perfect, his justice would be perfect. Of course, if god was perfect, his creation would be perfect too, unless he created it with inherent flaws in mind.

4) I don't worry too much about satan. Neither he nor his adversary actually exist.

You forgot to mention that God warned them that death would enter if they disobeyed Him.[63] I find the Genesis fall a great mystery. I have as many questions as you, if not more. There are also things in the Book of Kings and other books that make my hair stand on end. However, they don't stop me from loving God with all of my heart, serving Him with all of my strength, trusting Him with all my soul, and eagerly waiting for the Kingdom of God ... which is very close (when you look at the signs of the times).

A wise man once said, "Faith may swim, where reason may only paddle."

Bear with the following analogy: Two men are on a plane. Both have been warned that the plane will crash. They both have to jump 25,000 feet at any moment. They will perish if they don't obey the captain's words of warning. All four of the plane's engines are on fire.

One man has the good sense to put his parachute on. The other doesn't. He is incensed with the thought that the warning message that came over the speakers didn't come from the

63 "And the Lord God commanded the man, saying, Of every tree of the garden thou may freely eat: But of the tree of the knowledge of good and evil, thou shalt not eat of it: for in the day that you eat thereof you shall surely die" (Genesis 2:16-17).

captain. He thinks it was a recording and that the captain doesn't exist. His proof—the engines are on fire. If there was a captain, the engines wouldn't be in fire. Besides, the emergency instructions have stupid illustrations. Another reason he hasn't put on the parachute—the colors on the emergency instructions are not to his liking.

<<If god was perfect, his justice would be perfect. Of course, if god was perfect his creation would be perfect too, unless he created it with inherent flaws in mind.>>

True. Unless there's another explanation you haven't yet thought of.

64 This is available on a 16-CD message, and is called, "Common Objections to Christianity."

I conduct a seminar called, "God Doesn't Believe in Atheists."[64] In it, I have a number of questions and tests that show that we (as humans) are incredibly fallible. The tests are very humbling. There are not only many things we don't know, but we make stupid mistakes about things that we think we know.

Think about this for a moment. Just over one hundred years ago an educated man (who's name I have forgotten) said that humanity had uncovered everything there was to discover in creation. That was before air flight, the computer, the car, microwaves, the radio, the electric light, remote controls, etc., etc. I have learned never to think that I know everything ... especially when it comes to the attributes and ways of God. The Bible warns that His ways are not our ways. [65] God is nothing like we conceive Him to be. The Scriptures also say that we look through a "glass darkly." [66] They say that "we know in part." I will wait before I pass judgment.

Here's a small quote from the bible: 2 Kings 2:23—From there Elisha went up to Bethel. As he was walking along the road, some youths came out of the town and jeered at him. "Go on up, you baldhead!" they said. "Go on up, you baldhead!" He turned around, looked at them and called down a curse on them in the name of the Lord. Then two bears came out of the woods and mauled forty-two of the youths. And he went on to Mount Carmel and from there returned to Samaria.

Another bible I read referred to this as "Another of Elisha's Miracles." Miracle my [expletive]. I don't ally myself with murderers, whether they created what they killed or not. Despite all his power, god always seems to have to resort to murder to get his enemies out of the way. What do you think?

I have learned never to read God's Word at face value. Most[67] of that

[65] "Seek ye the LORD while he may be found, call ye upon him while he is near: Let the wicked forsake his way, and the unrighteous man his thoughts: and let him return unto the Lord, and he will have mercy upon him; and to our God, for he will abundantly pardon. For my thoughts are not your thoughts, neither are your ways my ways, says the LORD. For as the heavens are higher than the earth, so are my ways higher than your ways, and my thoughts than your thoughts"(Isaiah 55:6-9).

[66] "For now we see through a glass, darkly; but then face to face: now I know in part; but then shall I know even as also I am known" (I Corinthians 13:12).

43

67 I should have used the word, "much," in reference to the issue being addressed.

68 "Exactly what is a "type?" Theologically speaking, a "type" may be defined as "a figure or ensample of something future and more or less prophetic, called the 'Antitype'" (E. W. Bullinger, *Figures of Speech Used in the Bible*, p. 768). Muenscher says a type is "the preordained representative relation which certain persons, events, and institutions of the Old Testament bear to corresponding persons, events, and institutions in the New" (quoted in: M. S. Terry, *Biblical Hermeneutics,* p. 246). Wick Broomall has a concise statement that is helpful. "A type is a shadow cast on the pages of Old Testament history by a truth whose full embodiment or antitype is found in the New Testament revelation" (*Baker's Dictionary of Theology,* p. 533). We would, in summary, suggest the following definition, which we paraphrase from Terry. A type is a real, exalted happening in history which was divinely ordained by the omniscient God to be a prophetic picture of the good things which He purposed to bring to fruition in Christ Jesus." www.christiancourier.com/ archives/typology.htm

which is written in the Old Testament are Bible "types" of the New Testament.[68] Think of it like this. It seems that most of the things we value in this life have to be worked for: gold has to be dug up, diamonds, silver, etc. The Bible tells us that God "has hidden ... things from the wise and prudent."[69] Here's an example you may not be able to swallow, but here goes:

In the Gospel of John we are told that Peter pulled in a net containing 153 fish (see John 21:11). Why does Scripture make a point of giving the actual number? It's always been a mystery to me.

In the first chapter of 2 Kings, we are told that 51 soldiers were sent to arrest one man—Elijah. They were devoured by fire from Heaven. Another 51 were commissioned. They too were devoured by fire from Heaven. Another 51 men were sent out. This time the captain interceded on their behalf and saved them from Heaven's fire.

A total of 153 men were sent out. Two thirds perished. One third was saved because of the captain's intercession.

Some years before the catch of 153 fish, Jesus had told Peter that he would be a fisher of men (see Matthew 4:19). The Bible also tells us that in the Gospel net, the good fish and the bad fish sit alongside one another until they are sorted out on the Day of Judgment (see Matthew 13:47-50).[70] Those who are saved from Heaven's wrath are saved because of the ministry of the Captain of our Salvation (see Hebrews 10:2). He ever lives to make intercession for us (see Hebrews 7:25).

Do we have here an indication that two thirds of the professing Body of Christ will hear those terrifying words, "Depart from Me, you workers of iniquity. I never knew you" (Matthew 7:21)? Is this an indication that only one third will be saved? I don't know. One thing I do know is that around two thirds of the *contemporary* Body of Christ is lukewarm toward the lost, toward prayer, toward God's Word. Jesus warned that the lukewarm would be spewed out of His mouth (see Revelation 3:16).

Look at these verses from the Old Testament: "... 'Strike the shepherd, and the sheep will be scattered; then I will turn my hand against the little ones. And it shall come to pass in all the land,' says the Lord, 'That two-thirds shall be cut off and die, but one-third shall be left in it: I will bring the one-third through the fire, will refine them as silver is refined, and test them as gold is tested. They will call on my name, and I will answer them. I will say, 'This is my people'; and each one

69 "In that hour Jesus rejoiced in spirit, and said, I thank thee, O Father, Lord of heaven and earth, that thou hast hid these things from the wise and prudent, and hast revealed them unto babes: even so, Father; for so it seemed good in thy sight" "For it is written, I will destroy the wisdom of the wise, and will bring to nothing the understanding of the prudent" (Luke 10:21).

70 "Again, the kingdom of heaven is like unto a net, that was cast into the sea, and gathered of every kind: Which, when it was full, they drew to shore, and sat down, and gathered the good into vessels, but cast the bad away. So shall it be at the end of the world: the angels shall come forth, and sever the wicked from among the just, and shall cast them into the furnace of fire: there shall be wailing and gnashing of teeth" (Matthew 13:47-50).

will say, 'The Lord is my God'"
(Zechariah 13:7-9). In the light of the
fact that these verses refer to Jesus as
the smitten Shepherd (see Mark 14:27)
and can be applied to God's dealings
with the Church in refining it in fire as
gold is tested (see 1 Peter 1:7), I can't
help but be alarmed. I am also alarmed
that a vast multitude sit within the
Gospel net, thinking that they are
saved, when they don't have the things
that "accompany salvation." They
have named the name of Christ, but
have never departed from iniquity.
They call Jesus, Lord, but don't do the
things He tells them. The Lord is their
God, but their God isn't their Lord.
They will be the "many" who will cry
"Lord! Lord!" on Judgment Day, but
Jesus will say that He never knew[71]
them. They are hypocrites ... false
converts. They profess to know Him,
but they are in truth "workers of
iniquity." They are in the "sinning
Christian" category that so offend the
world ... and no doubt you. They
discredit Christianity with their lives.

**In regard to God always killing off His
enemies. You are still alive. Don't
tempt Him.**

* * *

One thing I thought I'd bring up about
your analogy—if there wasn't a
captain, the plane wouldn't be in the

[71] "Not every one that says unto me, Lord, Lord, shall enter into the kingdom of heaven; but he that does the will of my Father which is in heaven. Many will say to me in that day, Lord, Lord, have we not prophesied in your name? and in your name have cast out devils? and in your name done many wonderful works? And then will I profess unto them, I never knew you: depart from me, you that work iniquity" (Matthew 7:21-23).

air in the first place. You could of course use this to your advantage.

Now, I have an analogy for you to bear with. It's the way I see the flaw of creationist reasoning. Creationist reasoning says that the chances of life simply "occurring" are so slim, it would be impossible. Well, they're right—except they forgot to say "nearly impossible." The chances were so slim that it took trillions of years possibly until it finally happened with just the right balance on one little blue speck. Remember how I told you a while ago that while you may not win the lottery, someone does? Here's an analogy from that about how natural processes created the notion of creationism:

There is a lottery for 100 million dollars. 50 million people buy tickets. 48 million theists, if they won, would each thank god for his good grace. 1 person wins 100 million dollars. That person thanks the Lord. Proof enough, eh? THERE IS A GOD!!! 47,999,999 other theists pass it off as a statistical improbability anyway and go on with their lives. 2,000,000 atheists do the same thing.

I'm not a creationist then. I believe that the chances of life simply occurring are nil. Zilch. Non-existent. Zip. You get nothing from nothing.[72]

72 Even if it's left for a trillion years.

I have another little quote that is difficult to understand unless fully explained, but I'm not going to get into that right now. I'm going to try it out because I kind of set it up with my analogy, and I think you may just understand it (it's hard to understand because it's so vague). When the creationist talks about the statistical improbability of life forming without being created, I say: "If it hadn't happened just right, you wouldn't be here to wonder why it happened."

I hope you get that, as there's really no other way to put it. As a post script to it, you must also realize how many other planets may have formed the beginnings of life, but didn't have the right balance or didn't develop far enough along to ask the questions we as.

Wishing you the best, James D. Franz

* * *

But, the problem that I have found myself having with these statements is that they sound like built-in excuses put in by the writers of the bible to keep people from questioning too much. I put "faith" and "god works in mysterious ways" in that same category. There are a lot of excuses in religion that keeps itself, as you say, "axiomatic," in a manner of speaking.

I agree with you. Some people use "faith" and the "mysterious ways" thing as an intellectual copout when it comes to the Bible and the ways of God. But aren't we the same about life? Don't we have faith in our computers? Did you understand it before you used it? Don't you have faith in what you have been taught— what you "believe"? Doesn't nature itself work in "mysterious ways"? You just have to watch the Discovery Channel and see the marvels of nature to see the truth of that. Little bugs, etc., do incredible things to survive; the seasons, tides, etc., do things beyond human reasoning. We don't even know why we have to sleep. Give me some examples of the cop-outs that bug you and I will try my best to face them head-on.

* * *

<<It seems that most of the things we value in this life have to be worked for: gold has to be dug up, diamonds, silver, etc.>> This goes very well with a quote I made in rebuttal to a very similar statement long ago: "You can follow a map to just the right spot and begin digging for lost treasure, and if you don't find it, you can always dig deeper, but if there is no treasure, there you only prove to dig yourself into a hole."

I found the "treasure" on the 25th of April, 1:30 in the morning, 1972. See 2 Corinthians 4:7.

* * *

Has god created only to destroy? Why does he feel the need to cause such suffering as that which he has created in the fires of hell? What is the purpose of that? Why not just "uncreate" them? Does he feel the need to feed his own ego by proving to all these suffering souls just how powerful he is over them? I'm glad that I learned about the biblical version of god after I stopped believing, because it would have scared me terribly to have someone convince me it was all true. If god showed himself to me, proved his existence to me, that would not be my salvation if he were the god that the bible makes him out to be.

Proverbs 28:5 has the answer to this dilemma we find ourselves in. [73]

What exactly did happen on the 25th of April, 1:30 in the morning, 1972? I'd like to hear about it, honestly.

My mother was Jewish and because I had been born just after the Second World War, she was afraid that another Hitler might raise his ugly head, so my parents put "Methodist" on my birth certificate. In reality, I was given no instruction about God at all. During

[73] "Evil men understand not judgment: but they that seek the Lord understand all things" (Proverbs 28:5).

the 22 years of my non-Christian life, I only ended up in a church building three times. I found all three visits incredibly boring. The first time did have one highlight. A friend's parents made him go to church every Sunday. I was staying overnight, so I went with him. The boredom breaker was the wine that was passed around during communion. It tends to hit the back of the throat of a ten-year-old, and leave an impression.

When I was seven years old, an aunt taught me "The Lord's Prayer." That became a powerful sleeping pill. I couldn't go to sleep until I had rattled it off—I was addicted. But I could down that pill in nine seconds—from the "Our Father ... to the "Amen."

When I was thirteen, the Gideon's International came to our school and gave each of us a New Testament. I didn't hollow it out to keep drugs in it as others did. Instead, I took it home and read all of the Psalms. That kept me busy for 150 nights, one Psalm each night. That exercise did about as much for me as my three visits to church and the Lord's Prayer.

Around that time, I remember hearing a converted alcoholic testify on a street corner how he had had an experience with God. I thought that it was nice that he had found help with his problem.

I hardly had any thoughts about God (other than the nightly nine-second sleeping pill) until I was 18 years old. I was too busy to think of anything other than surfing. We lived opposite the beach, and I could see the surf from my bedroom. I had even made a flag that was raised by a well-trained mom when the daily dinner was ready.

Dinner was late one Saturday night, so I decided to have a quick surf. I had a brand new surfboard and I was still trying to break it in. I called my dog and headed for the beach. The animal was crazy, but went crazier when I mentioned the beach. He ran around in circles of joy. Chasing sea gulls meant as much to him as riding waves meant to me.

As we walked along the sidewalk, the thought of the joys of terrified gulls must have overtaken him. He ran ahead of me toward the beach. I called his name. No response. I called again as he ran across the road. Still no response. Suddenly, a car appeared from nowhere and struck the animal. He went underneath the vehicle and was thrust out the back. I was horrified. I dropped my new board on the sidewalk and ran out onto the road, picked up my beloved dog, ran home and sat at the end of our long driveway. Blood was dripping from his mouth and there was a hole in the unconscious animal's head. The car that had hit the dog stopped opposite the driveway. A distraught man got out, walked over to me, put one hand on my shoulder and burst into tears.

My older brother and I rushed the animal to the local veterinarian, where a day later they put him to sleep (the dog, that is).

That night I thought about God. Death tends to make us do that ... even if it's the death of a dog. The only other time I had such thoughts was when I lost a brand new underwater watch. It was winter, my hands were cold, and I must have unwittingly hit the side of my board as I paddled through the freezing water. When I suddenly saw that my watch was no longer on my wrist, I whispered, "My God ..." This was my brand new underwater watch that could go down to a depth of 600 feet. It had. I remember wondering why I instinctively said, "My God ..."

It was around October of 1971. Earlier that year I watched my friends risk their lives by jumping off a 50-foot cliff to kill boredom when there was no surf. One of them jumped first, to see how deep the water was. He came up with a bleeding nose, so from then on they only jumped when a wave rolled in. I refused to jump. I had gained an appreciation for life that was stronger than peer pressure.

It was because of this appreciation that I began to think deeply about the fact that one day it would end. Not only would my life end, but so would the lives of the ones I loved. It made no sense at all that everything I held dear to me was going to be ripped from my hands by something much greater than me—death. I was 21 years old, newly married, and had my own house, my own car and complete freedom to go where I wanted when I wanted. To say that I was happy was a gross understatement. However, I could see that my happiness bubble would be one day burst by the sharp pin of reality. It seemed an incredible enigma that the scientific and medical world were preoccupied with things that didn't really matter. They were worried about space exploration and finding a cure for the common cold, when death, like a great black cloud, was looming over them. They were straining a gnat, while being swallowed by a camel.

Surely, scientific and medical research should spearhead its energy into solving the great dilemma of death. Didn't they have the thoughts I was having? Were they quite happy to yield loved ones to the grave without a battle, or at least even a whimper of protest? It seemed no one talked openly about the subject. I kept such insane thoughts to myself.

I had been married for a year. Sue had just given birth to a baby boy and I wept for joy at the miracle of childbirth. The happiness bubble kept growing. I was so thankful for life and all that I had been blessed with, but I had no idea "who" I should thank. The thought that God had anything to do with blessing was far from my thoughts, even when I rattled off the Lord's Prayer each night.

When I checked with Sue about the possibility of going surfing with friends for a weekend, she didn't mind. That Friday afternoon, five of us left to drive 120 miles north of our city.

On the Saturday night of April 24th, 1972, I walked into Graeme and Wayne's room. Graeme was quietly sitting on his bed. Wayne was fast asleep. For some reason I sat down and began to talk. During that time, the subject of God surfaced. Wayne woke from a deep sleep and heard us talking about God. He aired his disapproval, and was so offended, he left the room.

Graeme and I spoke for 6 hours that night. During that time, I found myself confronted with the fact that I had violated the Ten Commandments. The Scripture that sunk like a sharp poison arrow into my heart was, "You have heard it said of old You shall not commit adultery. But I say unto you that whosoever shall look upon a woman to lust after her has committed adultery already with her in his heart" (Matthew 5:27, 28). It was the death of me. If God made my mind, he could see what He made ... He saw my thought-life. I was guilty of the sin of the heart a thousand times over. I knew that I would be condemned on Judgment Day and end up in Hell.

I was as trapped as a guilty criminal is the prison of Divine Justice. Suddenly, the door began to open. Jesus Christ, God in human form, came to this earth and suffered and died in my place. He took the punishment due to me. He paid my fine. He alone had the keys to death and Hell. For the first time in my life, the Gospel made sense to me. I found that the Bible says that the whole of creation was subjected to futility and death because of sin. When Jesus came to this earth, He took the curse of God upon Himself. That's why He bore the crown of thrones. That's why He died on the Cross. Then He rose from the dead and defeated death. I was told that night, if I would repent and trust in Jesus Christ, God would forgive my sins and give me the gift of everlasting life. Would I!

I asked God to forgive me for violating His Commandments. I gladly embraced the Savior as a man dying of thirst grasps a cup of water. It was then that I found the God who gave me life.

The only way I can even begin to describe the experience is to point to a newborn baby. It cries the moment it is born. If I could ask what the problem was, the baby may say, "Something is missing. I don't know what it is, but there is an instinctive cry in me that won't let up until I find what it is." The doctor then picks up the screaming child and places it upon the mother's breast. The baby stops crying and suckles. I tap the baby on its tiny shoulder and ask, "How do you feel now?" It looks at me with tears of joy in its wide eyes, and says, "This is it! This was what I was looking for. I had no idea what it was because I had never experienced it before."

On the night of April 25th, 1972, I found what I had been looking for. I had no idea what it was until the moment I experienced it. The Bible says that Jesus Christ shall make you "whole" (see Acts 9:34).

We went to bed at 3:30 that morning. As I drifted off to sleep, I had a fear that what I had found would be gone in the morning. It wasn't. In fact, it was so real, for the first time in ten years I didn't want to go surfing. I was quite happy to sit and read a Bible.

That was very strange. It was in there that I read of what had happened to me. The incredible peace I felt was what the Bible referred to as "peace that passes all understanding" (see Philippians 4:7). I didn't just feel peace; I felt like a new person. My eyes fastened on 2 Corinthians 5:17, "If any man be in Christ, he is a new creature; old things are passed away, behold, all things are become new." The Bible seemed to come alive as I read its words.

We told Brian, another surfing buddy who was with us, what had happened during the night. He was a Baptist by birth, but he hadn't been born again. He said that he desperately wanted whatever had happened to me, so that night, we tried to duplicated my experience. We waited until it became dark, went into the same room, turned down the light, and prayed. Nothing happened. Brian was very disappointed.

The following day, I went surfing. It was the best surf I had seen for the entire ten years of my surfing life. On reflection, it was a farewell gift.

It was about month after my conversion. I was still reeling at what had happened to me. I had truly been born again. I couldn't stop thinking about God and Jesus Christ. In the past, when I was on a phone, I would "doodle" by writing my name. After my conversion, with no forethought, I found myself writing the name of Jesus. I didn't understand it until I read in Scripture the words of Jesus, "When the Holy Spirit comes, He shall glorify Me" (John 16:14).

Over the previous months I had worked on a 50-minute surf movie called, "A Place of Our Own." Just before the premiere, someone gave me a copy of "The Son Worshippers," a documentary about the Jesus Revolution that was taking place in California. I gave myself a private screening on the wall of a spare room in my house. The producers had concluded the movie with one Bible verse. It said, "And you will know the truth, and the truth will make you free" (see John 8:32). I stared at the verse. It seemed to jump out at me. It was then that I began to grasp what it was that I was searching for before I became a Christian. It was "truth" that I was seeking. I was like a blind man groping for light. I had no idea why I was alive, what my purpose was in life, where I was going to or what death held for me. Now I knew the truth, and the truth had made me free. I decided that I would screen the 30-minute movie directly after the premiere of the surf movie, then share my testimony.

Three hundred excited surfers showed up to the premiere. They sat glued to their seats and watched "A Place of Our Own." Then I stood up and said, "I have another movie here. It's a much better production than the one you have just seen. It's about the Jesus Revolution in California." Suddenly about 150 surfers panicked and ran out of the hall. If I had hollered, "Fire!" they would have moved slower. I was thankful that at least 150 stayed, and then listened to me share how I had become a Christian. It was one of the hardest things I have ever had to do, but I knew that I had to do it if I cared about their eternal welfare.

I was mystified as to why so many would run out of a hall the moment they heard the name of Jesus. Once again, the Bible answered my question. The Scriptures say, "... men love darkness rather than light, because their deeds are evil. Neither will they come to the light, lest their deeds are exposed" (see John 3:20). Jesus said that the world would hate Him because He testified that their deeds were evil. [74] Criminals tend to flee from the law.

I would believe, obviously, but in my heart I would hate what he does, and I cannot change that.

That's the miracle of conversion. He takes the God-hating (the Bible says we hate God "without cause"),[75] blind, rebellious heart and transforms it. He

74 "The world cannot hate you; but me it hates, because I testify of it, that the works thereof are evil" (John 7:7).

75 "But this cometh to pass, that the word might be fulfilled that is written in their law, They hated me without a cause" (John 15:25). "Because the carnal mind is enmity against God: for it is not subject to the law of God, neither indeed can be (Romans 8:7).

did so with me, and He can with you. Criminals always hate justice.

I would be able to give my heart to Jesus, but then again it is said that Jesus and god are the same.[76] Why then does one turn the other cheek, yet the other gives the wrath of flames? Why is one loving and another is cruel?

Why does one seek out the sinners in order to help them, but one hides until the sinners come to him? Why does one try to strike peace while the other kills all his enemies?

Where did you get "give my heart to Jesus"? That's not in the Bible.[77] You have been duped by modern preachers.

There is no difference between the God of the Old Testament and Jesus in the New.

God told Israel to love strangers as themselves—see Leviticus 19:34.[78] Check out the wrath of Jesus Christ at His Second Coming—2 Thessalonians 1:7-9 … it's terrifying.[79]

* * *

<<"I am also alarmed that a vast multitude sit within the Gospel net, thinking that they are saved, when they don't have the things 'that

76 "In the beginning was the Word, and the Word was with God, and the Word was God. The same was in the beginning with God. All things were made by him; and without him was not any thing made that was made. And the Word was made flesh, and dwelt among us, (and we beheld his glory, the glory as of the only begotten of the Father,) full of grace and truth" (John 1:1-3, 14).

77 Salvation comes through "repentance towards God and faith towards our Lord Jesus Christ," rather than adding Jesus to a sinful lifestyle.

78 "But the stranger that dwells with you shall be unto you as one born among you, and thou shalt love him as thyself; for you were strangers in the land of Egypt: I am the LORD your God" (Leviticus 19:34).

79 "And to you who are troubled rest with us, when the Lord Jesus shall be revealed from heaven with his mighty angels, in flaming fire taking vengeance on them that know not God, and that obey not the gospel of our Lord Jesus Christ: Who shall be punished with everlasting destruction from the presence of the Lord, and from the glory of his power …" (II Thessalonians 1:7-9).

accompany salvation.' They have named the name of Christ, but have never departed from iniquity. They call Jesus Lord, but don't do the things He tells them. The Lord is their God, but their God isn't their Lord. They will be the 'many' who will cry 'Lord! Lord!' on Judgment Day, but Jesus will say that He never knew them. They are hypocrites ... false converts. They profess to know Him, but they are in truth 'workers of iniquity.' They are in the 'sinning Christian' category that so offend the world...and no doubt you.">>

You are very, VERY right about every point in this statement, right down to those last three words. There are so many, in fact too many who walk with righteous indignation and feel they are better than others simply because they follow Christianity. They think they're alright and set for eternity just because they SAY their prayers, when it takes a little more than just words to receive the grace of god. Their mouths speak it, but their hearts do not. Their lips mumble out the words while their minds swim in that for which they are asking forgiveness. They preach the gospel without using it. They go to church Sunday morning, but their hangover is keeping them from remembering the name of the girl they slept with last night. They follow the bible without having even laid a finger on it once in their life. True Christians they are not. True, very true. They disgust me as much as I'm sure they disgust you. [80]

It's kind of scary for me to know that a lot of christians aren't even as true to their beliefs as I am to mine! Sincerely, James D. Franz

P.S. Just thought I'd let you know that I've really been enjoying this discussion lately.

* * *

Let's think for a moment about a simple form of life. The fly. The "simple," common, everyday household fly. Let's say that there was no Creator. Let's believe that (what you say) "the chemicals on the cooled bodies possibly forming into life, and the balance and adaptation of that life to sustain and thrive and evolve into what we have now" is true.

There was nothing. I would now like to say that suddenly a big bang happened, but there is nothing to make a big bang, bang. Therefore we will we have to think in terms of a mysterious something before the big bang, making the big bang happen.

Let's reenact the Genesis of the evolutionary theory: "Bang!" or should I say "BANG!" After the big bang, we have the necessary

[80] It's interesting to note that the world hates hypocrisy. They don't want a godly person to be a fake. However, they are offended if a godly person *refuses* to be a hypocrite, and lives a life of holiness, loving righteousness and standing against sin. They scorn the hypocrite with an appearance of righteous indignation, while loving sin themselves. They will be judged with the same measure they judge. Look at what Scripture warns about those who look at the hypocrite and say that he sins: "And do you think this, O man, you who judge those practicing such things, and doing the same, that you will escape the judgment of God? Or do you despise the riches of His goodness, forbearance, and longsuffering, not knowing that the goodness of God leads you to repentance? But in accordance with your hardness and your impenitent heart you are treasuring up for yourself wrath in the day of wrath and revelation of the righteous judgment of God, who 'will render to each one according to his deeds': eternal life to those who by patient continuance in doing good seek for glory, honor, and immortality; but to those who are self-seeking and do not obey the truth, but obey unrighteousness indignation and wrath, tribulation and anguish, on

every soul of man who does evil, of the Jew first and also of the Greek; but glory, honor, and peace to everyone who works what is good, to the Jew first and also to the Greek. For there is no partiality with God" (Romans 2:3-11, NKJV).

(potential) raw materials (DNA) to make a fly. There are (potentially) two flaky very lightweight plastic membranes for the wings. There is also close at hand (potential) material that is able to form itself (over time) into two compound eyes. This will take some time (millions of years) because these are very complex (hundreds of tiny television screens, each with multiple nerve-endings). The eyes and the wings are living material, so they will need to be quickly connected (over millions of years) to the heart or they will frizzle and die. But wait. There is no blood yet. Some (potential) blood has fortunately come from of the big bang. We will also need blood vessels to carry the blood to the wings. Once these are connected, they will be able to grow into a mouth, brain (to flap the wings, etc.,), tongue, legs, skin, etc.

Suddenly, it all comes together into a male fly. Evolution has completed her work. The fly is finished. It will now need food and water to stay alive, but that's another theory. Now we just have to hope that a female fly has evolved at the same time over millions of years (with the necessary female reproductive parts), or there won't be any more flies.

But you say, "It didn't happen like that!" The beginning of what we know now as a fly began as a simple maggot-like form, then evolved into a fly ...

that took millions of years. How then does a maggot do it in a couple of days? Just one evolutionist has more faith than every Christian combined. I hope you are well. Ray

Well, okay, but keep in mind that the fly is not a simple form of life. You have a really bad example here.[81] The simplest life we have left is bacterium.[82] A fly is an intricately complex life form—don't let its size fool you.

I was being cynical. There are no simple forms of life. How can there be? The only simple thing in this life is the brain of a man who thinks that there are simple forms of life. If any form of life was simple, man could make it. He can't. With all his brain-power, he doesn't know how to.

Here's an example: Penguins. Penguins are birds, yet they can't fly. Penguins live in arctic regions, so cold that almost nothing else lives there. Penguins do not make much of a dent in the ecological cycle. If penguins went extinct, there would be no global consequences. Why do penguins exist? Why would a bird exist that can't fly, and live in such incredibly extreme temperatures? There are too many questions—penguins can't actually exist.

Here's your answer: God put them there. Why can't you accept that?

81 In other words, there's a possibility that evolution is feasible as long as it's not applied to something as complex as a fly.

82 Viruses are incredibly complex, but look at what an expert says about the complex nature of bacterium: "Bacteria are complex compared to viruses. A typical bacterium has a rigid cell wall and a thin, rubbery cell membrane surrounding the fluid, or cytoplasm, inside the cell. A bacterium contains all of the genetic information needed to make copies of itself—its DNA—in a structure called a chromosome. In addition, it may have extra loose bits of DNA called *plasmids* floating in the cytoplasm. Bacteria also have ribosomes, tools necessary for copying DNA so bacteria can reproduce." (See www.microbe.org/ microbesvirus_or_ bacterium.asp.)

83 "See how often science has altered its very basis. Science is notorious for being most scientific in destruction of all the science that has gone before it." (Charles Spurgeon)

There is good news for those who still have faith in science: "It's years into the new millennium, and the whole world of food has changed ... Americans are eating ... earthworm pizzas ... Experts say this country is at the beginning of what they predict will be a revolution in the food industry. The sky's the limit when it comes to what scientists can and probably will do, they say." *USA TODAY*, January 4, 1999.

84 Life's origins—the ever-changing mind of science. According to an NBC News report in August 1999, there was a "remarkable" discovery in Australia. They said the *Journal of Science* reported that they had found what they considered to be proof that life appeared on earth 2.7 billion years ago—a billion years earlier than previously thought. They now admit that they were wrong in their first estimate (a mere 1,000,000,000 years off), but with this discovery they are now sure that they have the truth ... until their next discovery. CBS News reported in October

<<There was nothing. I would now like to say that suddenly a big bang happened, but there is nothing to make a big bang, bang.>> The fact that we don't know "what caused" a big bang to "bang" does not disprove it. Creationists seem to think that all the unknowns, all the questions about evolution and the big bang that scientists are trying to answer somehow disprove the entire concept. You ask, "What caused the big bang," and I say, "I don't know." How do you expect anyone to know that? How do you expect science[83] today to know everything about two processes that are billions upon billions of years old?[84] In all the years of fossil digging, despite all the discoveries, we've barely gotten 7% of the total possible fossil record, and that's assuming their estimate for the total is correct—they underestimated, meaning we might not even have 1% of the fossil record![85]

If unanswered questions disproved ideas, then your belief would be untrue as well. I've asked you quite a few questions that you've responded to by saying you didn't know, and you've got a book to look that stuff up in that supposedly has all the answers!

A rock from Mars had bacteria fossils on it, fossils of life that were not from earth! Imagine that! Why why why why why why why? It must not be true.

What's to say a big bang needs something to start it anyway? Apparently your god didn't need a start, and that's an intelligence with the power to create such things as natural laws, time, matter energy intelligence biology DNA RNA heaven hell and everything in between. In your reality, anything is possible because everything that is possible can never be as complex or as improbable as that which created the reality!

<< Therefore will we have to think in terms of a mysterious something before the big bang, making the big bang happen. >> No, it just happened. That's the best way to put it. As I asked before, why should everything have a reason for happening? There are two questions to most occurrences: "How?" and "Why?" The "how" just takes time, but unless you're dealing with life, or something with the ability to make choices, there is usually no "Why?" You can ask it over and over, but there often isn't an answer. Like penguins—you could ask, "Why?" about penguins and get nowhere fast. There are answers to "How?" But penguins don't have a reason for existing. They just do. The meteor that struck Jupiter—something must have caused that! There must be a reason! Why?!?!? There is no "Why?" It just happened.

1999 that discoveries were made of the bones of an unknown animal in Asia that may be as much as 40 million years old. This changed scientific minds as to *where* man first originated. Scientists once believed that primates evolved in Africa, but now they think they may be wrong, and that man's ancestors may have originated in Asia. So they believe ... until the next discovery. *USA Today* (March 21, 2001) reported, "Paleontologists have discovered a new skeleton in the closet of human ancestry that is likely to force science to revise, if not scrap, current theories of human origins." Reuters reported that the discovery left "scientists of human evolution ... *confused*," saying, "Lucy may not even be a direct human ancestor after all."

What is science? "We are invited, brethren, most earnestly to go away from the old-fashioned belief of our forefathers because of the supposed discoveries of science. What is science? The method by which man tries to hide his ignorance. It should not be so, but so it is. You are not to be dogmatical in theology, my brethren, it is wicked; but for scientific men it is the correct thing. You are never to assert anything very strongly; but scientists may boldly assert what they cannot prove, and may demand a faith far more credulous than any we possess. Forsooth, you and I are to take our Bibles and shape and mould our belief according to the ever-shifting teachings of so-called scientific men. What folly is this! Why, the march of science, falsely so called, through the world may be traced by exploded fallacies and abandoned theories. Former explorers once adored are now ridiculed; the continual wreckings of false hypotheses is a matter of universal notoriety. You may tell where the supposed learned have encamped by the debris left behind of suppositions and theories as plentiful as broken bottles." (Charles Spurgeon)

85 "Fossils are a great embarrassment to Evolutionary theory and offer strong support for the concept of Creation." (Dr. Gary Parker, Ph.D., Biologist/paleontologist and former Evolutionist) *"The number of fossils in some areas is enormous. How could earth have supported all those creatures at the same time?"* This question shows a common false assumption that many people make. They assume the earth today is the same as it has always been. Today's earth is seventy percent under water. There are scriptural

<< Let's reenact the Genesis of the evolutionary theory: "Bang!" or should I say "BANG!" >> Actually, scientists are agreed that if it were typed out, the big bang would be no less than eleven inches in length, seven inches high, and most likely (from astronomical and telemetric data compared between the Andromeda system and RT-6295) in Times New Roman, 72 point font. :)

<< After the big bang we have the necessary (potential) raw materials (DNA) to make a fly. There are (potentially) two flaky very lightweight plastic membranes for the wings. There is also close at hand (potential) material that is able to form itself (over time) into two compound eyes. >> You are grossly over simplifying to make the idea sound silly. In the ears of someone who actually understands the process, though (at least as best humans can so far), you are the one who sounds silly. Hold on—I'll deal with this in a moment.

<< This will take some time (millions of years) because these are very complex (hundreds of tiny television screens, each with multiple nerve-endings). >> Hey, maybe you have studied evolution. You say it would have to take millions of years, well guess what? There were billions for it all to happen! So, what was god doing during all that time? Twiddling his

thumbs? I would accept that he was guiding evolution, creating his masterpiece, but that would be absence of omnipotence, wouldn't it? And, he apparently spent millions upon millions of years fooling around, tinkering with dinosaurs[86] until he realized they didn't have any potential and decided to kill them all off. Or, are you one of those who say that the universe is no more than 6,000 years old and that god (or satan) planted the fossil record and all the other evidence to give the appearance of age (as well as speeding up the light from other stars to reach us so it wouldn't take the millions of years it does take). If you think that's a crazy idea, well, there are christians who believe it, and it's their only explanation for the evidence on this earth. Hope this has helped, James D. Franz

Now who has blind, unquestioning faith? If you leave God out of the equation, you are going to have "why's" all over the place. You don't even know why you exist. Tell me if you can. What is the reason ... the purpose for your existence?

No one ever said there was nothing. As you have heard me say over and over, there had to be something in the beginning (if you want to call it a "beginning," as that is just a human ideal). I say there was energy. You say there was god.[87] There's not all that

and scientific indications that the pre-Flood world had greater air pressure, higher percentages of oxygen and carbon dioxide, much more land (above sea level), less water (on the earth's surface), and a canopy of water to filter out the harmful effects of the sun. This would cause there to be many times more plants and animals on the earth than there are today. The added air pressure would diffuse more gasses into the water and support a much greater fish population. Aquatic plant life per cubic mile would multiply also. Second Peter 3 tells us that the scoffers in the last days will be willingly ignorant of how God created the heavens and the earth. They would also be ignorant of the Flood. These two great events must be considered before making any statements about the conditions on earth today. Only about three percent of the earth today is habitable for man. The rest is under water, ice, deserts, mountains, etc. If the earth before the Flood were, say, seventy percent habitable, it could have supported a huge population. The vast amount and worldwide distribution of fossils shows that the Flood was global and that God hates sin enough to judge the entire world." (Dr. Kent Hovind)

"About 85 percent of the rock surface around the world is made up of sedimentary rock, indicating that at some time in the past, the world was covered by water." Peter and Paul Lalonde, *301 Startling Proofs & Prophecies* (From *The Evidence Bible*).

86 "Did dinos soar? Imaginations certainly took flight over *Archaeoraptor Liaoningensis*, a birdlike fossil with a meat-eater's tail that was spirited out of northeastern China, 'discovered' at a Tucson, Arizona, gem and mineral show in 1999, and displayed at the National Geographic Society in Washington, D.C. Some 110,000 visitors saw the exhibit, which closed January 17; millions more read about the find in November's *National Geographic*. Now, paleontologists are eating crow. Instead of 'a true missing link' connecting dinosaurs to birds, the specimen appears to be a composite, its unusual appendage likely tacked on by a Chinese farmer, not evolution. (Sloan, C.P., "Feathers for T. Rex?", *National Geographic* 196 (5):98-107, November, 1999)

"*Archaeoraptor* is hardly the first 'missing link' to snap under scrutiny. In 1912, fossil remains of an ancient hominid were found in England's Piltdown quarries and quickly dubbed man's apelike ancestor. It took decades to reveal the

much difference between what we believe. Except I believe intelligence had to come about. You say it has always been.

You are saying that there was energy in the beginning, but the energy had no intelligence. Then the dumb energy brought about intelligence. That's not intelligent at all.

<< "I have found Him faithful to every promise He has made.">> Have any examples handy?[88]

He gave me life (twice).
He supplied my every need.
He gave me a wife.
He gave me healthy children.
He gave me friends.
He gave me everlasting life.
He gave me a Book of promises.
He gave me a massive Christian family of millions of people.
He gave me peace that passes understanding
He gave me joy unspeakable.
He gave me health.
He gave me eyes.
He brought me to this nation.
He gave me the beauty of His creation.
He has never left me, nor will He ever leave me.
He gave me power over my fears.
He took the sting out of death.
He proved His love towards me through the Cross.

He opened my blind eyes to His reality.
He took me out of darkness.
He saved my children from death.
He trusted me with a wonderful ministry.
He gave me the ability to speak for Him.
He showed me how foolish atheism is (See Psalm 14:1).[89]

"Though He slay me, yet will I trust Him" (Job 13:15).

"Great is thy faithfulness.
Great is Thy faithfulness.
Morning by morning, new mercies I see.
All that I needed, Thy hands have provided.
Great is Thy faithfulness, Lord unto me."

I would not want to have to live for eternity. Perhaps you've never thought about it, but eternity is a long time. A very long time. I wouldn't want to live knowing that I will be conscious forever.

That shows how miserable you are.[90] Admit it. You are bored ... unless you are lying and don't want to die. I am longing for eternity. No more pain, suffering, disease, death, or dandruff. I love my life, and I can't wait for God's Kingdom to come. All the biblical signs of the end of this age are

hoax." (*U.S. News & World Report*, February 14, 2000) "Darwin admitted that millions of 'missing links,' transitional life forms, would have to be discovered in the fossil record to prove the accuracy of his theory that all species had gradually evolved by chance mutation into new species. Unfortunately for his theory, despite hundreds of millions spent on searching for fossils worldwide for more than a century, the scientists have failed to locate *a single missing link* out of the millions that must exist if their theory of evolution is to be vindicated." Grant R. Jeffery, *The Signature of God*. "There are gaps in the fossil graveyard, places where there should be intermediate forms, but where there is nothing whatsoever instead. No paleontologist ... denies that this is so. It is simply a fact. Darwin's theory and the fossil record are in conflict." (David Berlinsky) "Scientists concede that their most cherished theories are based on embarrassingly few fossil fragments and that huge gaps exist in the fossil record." *Time* magazine, Nov. 7, 1977. "The evolutionists seem to know everything about the missing link except the fact that it is missing." (G.K. Chesterton, from *The Evidence Bible*.)

87 "In the beginning God created the heaven and the earth. And the earth was without form, and void; and darkness was upon the face of the deep. And the Spirit of God moved upon the face of the waters. And God said, Let there be light: and there was light" (Genesis 1:1-3).

88 Ask an unsaved person what God has done for them, and often they will not be able to think of anything. Yet, He gave them their blood, skin, bones, heart, liver, kidneys, lungs, eyes, ears, nose, mouth, hair, hands, feet, and their brain. He gave us life itself, and sustains the breath in our nostrils. The Bible asks the rhetorical question, "And what do you have that you did not receive?" (1 Corinthians 4:4).

89 "The fool has said in his heart, There is no God. They are corrupt, they have done abominable works, there is none that does good" (Psalm 14:1).

90 *Miserable* from the Latin, meaning "pitiable."

91 There are many prophecies that say that these times (the "end of the age") would see an increase in wars (Matthew 24:6), disease (Matthew 24:7), earthquakes (Matthew 24:7), religious cults (Matthew 24:5),

lined up perfectly. The daily news reads like a page of the Bible. [91] I feel sorry for you, having a death wish. Next thing you will be making an appointment with Doctor Death to put you to sleep. Still, the futility in which you live is of your own making. You don't have to stay in darkness. It's your choice.

It seems to me that you think that God has a ghostly existence awaiting those who trust in Him (<< knowing that I will be conscious forever>>). How wrong that is. He will give a new body to all that trust in His mercy. [92] We will live on earth ... an earth that will have the curse lifted off it. Hey, all this stuff is provable. All you have to do is humble yourself, repent, trust in Jesus and He will reveal Himself to you. See John 14:21—it's either true or it isn't. [93]

Life duplicates itself every day—an amazing feat in itself! What's to say it didn't develop on its own over an incredibly unfathomable amount of time?

Time rots things. It's called "entropy"— "The irreversible tendency of a system, including the universe, toward increasing disorder." Name something that doesn't rot, break down, crumble, etc., over millions of years. The law of entropy disproves the entire "time creates stuff" argument.

<< You don't even know why you exist. Tell me if you can. What is the reason ... the purpose for your existence? >> My purpose is what I make of it. That's the great thing about life—happiness is directly proportional to the amount of work you put into it. Purpose is about the same thing. But, I see no natural purpose which existed for me before I was able to decide what that purpose would be. The idea of a "purpose" or a "reason" are human ideals, and ideals which religion seems to offer, which is one of the many reasons for the perseverance in the idea of god.

But, I've noticed that the "purpose" theism offers is specious in nature, "specious" meaning that it superficially appears plausible, or it looks good, but upon close inspection is found to be flawed or inconsistent.

What, if you can tell me, is your purpose for existence? You like to ask why, so keep asking yourself that. After you've found your purpose, try and see what kind of purpose that achieves, and work your way backward up that ladder, continuing to ask what the purpose of all your purposes is. What does it all achieve? What is the purpose in all of it, after all things are considered? Let me know, James D. Franz

occult activity (2 Timothy 4:1), persecution of Christians (Matthew 24:9), the gospel will be preached (Matthew 24:14), violence would increase (Matthew 24:37), famines (Matthew 24:7), signs in the sun (Luke 21:25), a homosexual increase (2 Timothy 3:3), a great fear of the future (Luke 21:25), stress leading to heart attacks (Luke 21:26), materialism (2 Timothy 3:1, 4), denial of the Noahic flood (2 Peter 3:5-6), turning away from biblical truth to fables (2 Timothy 4:4—perhaps a reference to Santa Claus instead of Jesus Christ at Christmas, and the fable of the evolution theory instead of the biblical account of creation), immorality (Matthew 24:12), rebellious youth (2 Timothy 3:2), hypocrisy (2 Timothy 3:5), a forsaking of marriage (1 Timothy 4:3), a dead religious system (2 Timothy 3:5), a forsaking of the Ten Commandments (Matthew 24:12), vegetarianism (2 Timothy 4:3), money-grubbing preachers who will slur the Christian faith (2 Peter 2:1-2), the Jewish possession of Jerusalem (Luke 21:24—fulfilled in 1967), the city of Jerusalem becoming a burden to the nations (Zechariah 12:3), etc. Another sign is that skeptics (in their ignorance) would say that these signs have always been around (2 Peter 3:4).

92 "Behold, I show you a mystery; We shall not all sleep, but we shall all be changed, In a moment, in the twinkling of an eye, at the last trump: for the trumpet shall sound, and the dead shall be raised incorruptible, and we shall be changed. For this corruptible must put on incorruption, and this mortal [must] put on immortality. So when this corruptible shall have put on incorruption, and this mortal shall have put on immortality, then shall be brought to pass the saying that is written, Death is swallowed up in victory. O death, where is your sting? O grave, where [is] your victory?" (1 Corinthians 15:51-55) "Who shall change our vile body, that it may be fashioned like unto his glorious body, according to the working whereby he is able even to subdue all things unto himself" (Philippians 3:21). "Beloved, now are we the sons of God, and it doth not yet appear what we shall be: but we know that, when he shall appear, we shall be like him; for we shall see him as he is" (1 John 3:2).

93 "He that has my commandments, and keeps them, he it is that loves me: and he that loves me shall be loved of my Father, and I will love him, and will manifest

You didn't tell me what the purpose of your existence is. You merely told me what you do with your time.

We were created by God, for His pleasure. [94] Our pleasure is His pleasure. No, we are not His "play things." Do you have children? Does their pleasure give you pleasure? Are they your play things? In parenthood, we catch a tiny glimpse of the relationship we should have with the God who becomes our Father, the moment we are born into His family.

James—I wouldn't lie to you (see Revelation 21:8). [95] I mean what I am going to say. I love my wife with all of my heart. We have lived and worked together for 27 years.[96] (We are rarely apart.) We have a wonderful marriage. When I travel, I call her—up to ten times in a weekend. But I love God more than I love her. I love Sue 100 percent. I love God even more. She is the gift, God is the Giver. If God was some religious "idea," why would I say such a thing? I'm not a simpleton. I am a skeptic—not easily duped. I would never join a cult. So why would I say such a strange thing?

"Why do you believe everything has to have a designer, but then totally ignore that belief with god? Is it just because the bible says so, or what?"

Name something that you own that had no maker.

Miserable? Sorry, you're making baseless assumptions again.

These are your words: "I would not want to have to live for eternity." You don't want to have to live for eternity ... that means you don't value, enjoy or appreciate your life. Actually, the Bible says that you are already dead.[97] Did you know that? Until God "quickens" us (makes us alive through the new birth), death is at work in us. It says that we are in darkness and that our life is futile. [98] Your words testify to that truth.

Do you want to change the wording and say something like: "When I try and comprehend 'eternity,' it blows me away. It seems like such a long time." You think like that, because you are not born of the Spirit. We are not going to be stuck in an elevator forever ... then eternity would be unbearable.

The human mind thrives on challenges. God owns all of the universe ... those that love Him will never know boredom again. Once again I have the frustrating problem of trying to explain light to a blind man.

I hope you don't ever read any of my letters with a harsh tone. They're not

myself to him" (John 14:21).

94 "You are worthy, O Lord, to receive glory and honor and power: for you have created all things, and for your pleasure they are and were created" (Revelation 4:11).

95 "But the fearful, and unbelieving, and the abominable, and murderers, and whoremongers, and sorcerers, and idolaters, and all liars, shall have their part in the lake which burns with fire and brimstone: which is the second death" (Revelation 21:8).

96 Written in 1998.

97 "And you has he quickened, who were dead in trespasses and sins; even when we were dead in sins, has quickened us together with Christ" (Ephesians 2:1, 5).

98 "For the creature was made subject to vanity, not willingly, but by reason of him who has subjected [the same] in hope, because the creature itself also shall be delivered from the bondage of corruption into the glorious liberty of the children of God. For we know that the whole creation groans and travails in pain together until now" (Romans 8:20-22).

99 "But the natural man receives not the things of the Spirit of God: for they are foolishness unto him: neither can he know them, because they are spiritually discerned" (1 Corinthians 2:14).

100 "But as it is written, Eye has not seen, nor ear heard, neither have entered into the heart of man, the things which God has prepared for them that love him" (1 Corinthians 2:9).

written that way. (I try to keep away from "yelling-marks"—!!!) God bless, Ray

<<You are bored ... unless you are lying and don't want to die.>> Bored? Well, let's see—did I say I want to die right now, get it all over with? No, I said I wouldn't want to live for eternity. I'm fascinated by my life, and I hope that in the amount of time I potentially have that I get to accomplish everything I set out to do. But, I do eventually want to die. I wouldn't mind if life was a little longer, like maybe a few hundred years or maybe even a thousand, but I definitely would one day want to die. I'm not miserable, and I'm not bored, and I don't have a death wish. Sometimes your ability to understand leaves much to be desired.

<< I am longing for eternity. No more pain, suffering, disease, death or dandruff.>> Living in a fantasy.[99] Fantasies are always just perfect, aren't they? Well, list me an infinite number of activities that you plan to fill eternity with, and I'll believe you're prepared to never truly die.[100]

<< I feel sorry for you, having a death wish. Next thing you will be making an appointment with Doctor Death to put you to sleep.>> I feel sorry for you, living with such outlandish expectations of reality. I have no death wish. I simply don't want to live forever.

<< It seems to me that you think that God has a ghostly existence awaiting those that trust in Him. ("knowing that I will be conscious forever"). How wrong that is. He will give a new body to all that trust in His mercy. We will live on earth ... an earth that will have the curse lifted off it. >> I don't think god has any sort of existence awaiting us.

Hey, all this stuff is provable.

SO PROVE IT!!!

<< Still, the futility in which you live is of your own making. >> Futility? You may not stoop to name-calling, but you've really made yourself out to be an [expletive] in this letter.

I don't get why this upsets you. Anyway, that's a good sign. When a dentist touches a raw nerve, it shows him that there's a problem.

What I said was true. You should be thankful that you have a friend who cares enough to risk offending you by telling you the truth. Isn't it true that you, by an act of your own will, chose not to repent and trust the Savior?

<< He gave me everlasting life. >> But, we won't find out until we die, of course.

101 "And this is the record, that God has given to us eternal life, and this life is in his Son. He that has the Son has life; and he that has not the Son of God has not life. These things have I written unto you that believe on the name of the Son of God; that you may know that you have eternal life, and that you may believe on the name of the Son of God" (1 John 5:11-13)

102 "For the wisdom of this world is foolishness with God. For it is written, He takes the wise in their own craftiness" (1 Corinthians 3:19).

James, I cannot emphasize this enough. I KNOW I have everlasting life.[101] You will have to confine your "we" to yourself. You, because of your willful ignorance (there's no nice way to put this), will find out at your death that you were wrong. There will be no second chance for you. The Bible says that God "takes the wicked in their own craftiness."[102] He knows the real reason for your rebellion. It's your love for sin. Why don't you admit it? Your "atheism" and "evolution theory" are just thin bushes you hide behind. You don't even fool me, because I have been where you are now.

If you do die in your sins (God forbid), and your eyes meet my eyes on Judgment Day, I'm free from your blood. I have warned you that God will punish every sin, including every secret sin of the heart.

* * *

So, if you agree with entropy, you agree the natural system of the universe is in disorder, right?

No. It *tends* to disorder. Big difference. There is order throughout the entire universe, but it is rotting/breaking down, crumbling. You still didn't name something that doesn't rot, break down, crumble, etc. over millions of years. You seemed to have evaded the question.

<< Name something that doesn't rot, break down, crumble, etc. over millions of years. >> That's funny, you know, I can really only name two things—biological material (life) and radioactive decay. Can you think of any more examples? The basic materials for everything don't break down; they change forms.

Sorry. All life dies, including "biological material." Radioactive decay is "decay." It *has* broken down.

* * *

So then what is the purpose of hell? It obviously can't be justice, because no one could ever hope to commit an act which is deserving of such torture. Is our suffering also his pleasure? Does he feel the need to punish people because they don't please him, or is there another reason?

Does a judge get pleasure when he sends a murderer to prison? Perhaps. I know that relatives rejoice when the person who murdered a loved one is punished. I suppose you think murderers shouldn't be punished. Let me know your thoughts about that.

Jesus taught to turn the other cheek,[103] which is far from what god ever did.

God was in Christ reconciling the world to Himself.[104]

103 "You have heard that it has been said, An eye for an eye, and a tooth for a tooth: But I say to you, That you resist not evil: but whosoever shall smite you on your right cheek, turn to him the other also. And if any man will sue you at the law, and take away your coat, let him have your cloke also. And whosoever shall compel you to go a mile, go with him two. Give to him that asks you, and from him that would borrow of you turn not thou away. You have heard that it has been said, You shall love your neighbor, and hate your enemy. But I say to you, Love your enemies, bless them that curse you, do good to them that hate you, and pray for them which despitefully use you, and persecute you; That you may be the children of your Father which is in heaven: for he makes his sun to rise on the evil and on the good, and sends rain on the just and on the unjust" (Matthew 5:38-45).

104 "… God was in Christ, reconciling the world unto himself, not imputing their trespasses unto them; and has committed unto us the word of reconciliation" (2 Corinthians 5:19).

105 The assumptions made in the movie were not scientific, but came from the over-active imaginings of Hollywood screen-writers.

* * *

<< **Name something that you own that had no maker.** >> Keep in mind that what I name I name from my own beliefs. In your beliefs, everything has a maker, so in your mind I can't name anything. But, here are some things I own without human designers, at least:

A chunk of amber with an insect trapped inside, like in Jurassic Park[105] (no DNA though). Of course, the amber was "made" by a tree, so let's try something else. The air in my lungs. A rock shaped almost exactly like an egg (incredibly smoothed, too). A quartz crystal. A fuzzy rock—crystalline formations on its surface which are so thin they feel like hair. The dirt and rock directly beneath my house. The water I drink. The food I eat. The trees in my yard.

I couldn't really list anything living, because then you could claim they were made by their predecessors, as even trees grow from seeds. Therefore, the only purely natural things that could be listed are things such as rocks, basic elements, natural compounds, and other such things. Anything else either found a way to be developed or were designed by what developed.

Of all the things in your world, all of those complex creations that need a designer, I can list one major thing that doesn't have a designer, yet it's more complex than every other creation in that universe: your god.

If something as great and complex as your god requires no designer, why do you think anything does?

Sorry, God made all that stuff—air, rock, food, and water.[106] **I'm serious— use your imagination. Name something material you own that wasn't made.**

<<These are your words: "I would not want to have to live for eternity." You don't want to have to live for eternity ... that means you don't value, enjoy or appreciate your life. >> Let's compare: I don't want to have to live for eternity. I don't appreciate my life.

Those two sound very different. I value and appreciate and enjoy my life very much, and I would also love to live it a lot longer than the time we get on earth, but I know that one day out of those infinite number of days that you say we have ahead of us, I will not want to continue anymore.

I value and appreciate and enjoy my life BECAUSE it will end.

You stop valuing something after you realize so fully that you can never lose

[106] "All things were made by him; and without him was not any thing made that was made" (John 1:3).

it—that's what I'm afraid of. I don't want to lose that appreciation.

<< I KNOW I have everlasting life. >> Simple question: How do you know? Be specific, please.

Imagine for a moment that I said that I would give you $10,000,000 next week at this time. As a token of good faith, I will give you $1,000,000 right now, and put it in your hand. You could rightly conclude that I would keep my word because I wouldn't have given you $1,000,000 if I hadn't meant it.

God promises all who trust in Him everlasting life. As a token of good faith He gives us "the earnest of the Spirit." That was my experience 27 years ago next April.

There's more. A little child was looking at a heater. His dad says, "Don't touch that heater; it's hot." At that point, the child believes the heater is hot. Dad goes out of the room. He reaches out his hand to see if it really is hot. The moment his flesh burns, he stops believing the heater is hot. He now KNOWS it's hot. He's moved out of the realm of belief into the realm of experience.

For 22 years, I believed in God's existence. I wasn't a "fool" (see Psalm 14:1). I knew that that which was made, had a maker. The night I was saved, I touched the heater bar of God's love and forgiveness and passed out of the realm of belief into the realm of experience.

Think back to the child. In comes a heater expert and says, "You couldn't have been burned. I'm an expert. I have degrees in heaters ..." :) He can't persuade the child, because the child knows what he experienced.

The man with an experience is not at the mercy of a man who merely has an argument—"But you will receive power when the Holy Spirit comes upon you" (Acts 1:8), "When the Gospel came not unto you in word only, but in power, in the Holy Spirit and in much assurance" (1 Thessalonians 1:5), "You will know that you have passed from death unto life ..." (1 John 3:14).

* * *

So, you want me to just come out and give away my secret? That I actually do believe in god, but I'm hiding it behind unbelief out of psychological need to escape prosecution for my sins? Yeah, right. Just because I don't believe in god doesn't mean I love sin. There are a few sins I do like, namely sexual contact, but it doesn't have to be a sin, if I'm married at the time. Other than that, well, let's see:

1. "You shall have no other gods before Me." I have no gods before Him.

2. "You shall not make for yourself any graven image." Haven't done that.

3. "You shall not take the name of the Lord your God in vain." Don't do that.

4. "Remember the Sabbath Day, to keep it holy." Well, I work Mon-Fri now, but I still try to get errands done on Sunday.

5. "Honor your father and your mother." I do this every day—I love both of them dearly.

6. "You shall not murder." Never did this, have no desire to, wouldn't wish death on anyone (very divided over capital punishment issue, but don't feel I'll ever directly deal with it anyway).

7. "You shall not commit adultery." Well, I'm not married, which is technically what adultery is, but if you want to expand this to just sex outside of marriage, of that I am guilty (though not for over a year now).

8. "You shall not steal." I've done this (slight kleptomaniac tendencies) long ago, but have no desire to anymore, and I have not stolen anything in a long time.

9. "You shall not bear false witness." I have lied, and possibly have recently, which I must admit to. I don't enjoy lying, I can tell you that.

10. "You shall not covet." I don't do this. I don't want a lot in my life when it comes to material goods. The things I want most can't be bought, and definitely can't be found at anyone's house.

Well, I do enjoy sex, I admit, but it doesn't have to be a sin. Well, I can't see where exactly I love sin. Could you kindly point this out for me, Ray?

James, I am delighted that you took the time to go through the Ten Commandments. That is the standard with which God will judge you (see Romans 2:12, James 2:12)[107] and the only means by which we may know God's standards (see Romans 7:7).[108] Without God's Law (as it is called) we make the tragic mistake of judging ourselves by our own standards, rather than God's.

You have kindly given me your response to each Commandment, so I will now give you the biblical response ... if that's O.K.

<< 1. "You shall have no other gods before Me." I have no gods before Him. >>

107 "For as many as have sinned without law shall also perish without law: and as many as have sinned in the law shall be judged by the law" (Romans 2:12). "So speak ye, and so do, as they that shall be judged by the law of liberty" (James 2:12).

108 "What shall we say then? is the law sin? God forbid. No, I had not known sin, but by the law: for I had not known lust, except the law had said, Thou shalt not covet" (Romans 7:7).

This is what it means to put God first in your life (to have no other gods before Him): You shall love the Lord your God with all of your heart, mind, soul, and strength. You are also commanded to love your neighbor (every other human being) as much as you love yourself. In fact, Jesus said that your love for God should be so great that your love for your family and your own life should seem like hatred, compared to the love that you have for the God who gave those loved ones and your life to you. [109] No one can say that he has kept that Commandment.

<< 2. "You shall not make for yourself any graven image." Haven't done that. >>

You have committed the most common of sins with your "idolatry." You created your own god in your mind as a child, didn't like what you created, so you got rid of the image. Now you deny that which is axiomatic. You deny the inner light that God has given you (see John 1:9).[110] Idolatry is the greatest sin of all because it opens the door to transgression of the other Commandments. Why do you think we live in such a sinful nation, filled with murder, adultery, rape, greed, lying, and stealing? Simply because America has made a god in its own image.

109 "If any man come to me, and hate not his father, and mother, and wife, and children, and brethren, and sisters, yea, and his own life also, he cannot be my disciple" (Luke 14:26).

110 "That was the true Light, which lights every man that comes into the world" (John 1:9).

<< 3. "You shall not take the name of the Lord your God in vain." Don't do that. >>

This means that we should honor God's holy name. Godly Jews won't even *speak* His name because it is so holy. When a man substitutes it for a four-lettered word to express disgust, he is blaspheming the Name of the God who gave him life. You have the right to remain silent. However, everything you say will be taken down and may be used as evidence against you—"every idle word a man speaks, he shall give an account thereof on the Day of Judgment." The Bible also warns, "The Lord will not hold him guiltless, who takes His Name in vain."

<< 4. "Remember the Sabbath Day, to keep it holy." Well, I work Monday-Friday now, but I still try to get errands done on Sunday. >>

I went for 22 years as a non-Christian, knowing that God gave me life, and never once did I ask, "What do you require of me ... one day in seven?" I violated that Commandment many times.

Have you ever given a child a gift and he's snatched it from your hands and walked off? Ingratitude is a horrible thing. Never once did I thank God for my food. I must have looked like an ungrateful, selfish brat. A few weeks in Ethiopia would have put some gratitude in my heart.

<< 5. "Honor your father and your mother." I do this every day—I love both of them dearly. >>

This means to value them implicitly. It means to never have a bad attitude towards them, even once. I blew that many times with a selfish attitude in my teenage years.

<< 6. "You shall not murder." Never did this, have no desire to, wouldn't wish death on anyone (very divided over capital punishment issue, but don't feel I'll ever directly deal with it anyway). >>

Jesus said that if we get angry without cause, we are in danger of Judgment[111] … the Bible also says, "Whoever hates his brother is a murderer."[112] No one who has ever driven on a freeway could say he is innocent.

<< 7. 'You shall not commit adultery.' Well, I'm not married, which is technically what adultery is, but if you want to expand this to just sex outside of marriage, that I am guilty (though not for over a year now).>>

Jesus said, "Whoever looks upon a woman to lust after her has committed

111 "But I say unto you, That whosoever is angry with his brother without a cause shall be in danger of the judgment: and whosoever shall say to his brother, Raca, shall be in danger of the council: but whosoever shall say, Thou fool, shall be in danger of hell fire" (Matthew 5:22).

112 See 1 John 3:15.

adultery already with her in his heart."[113] Sex out of and before marriage is considered to be adultery (see Matthew 5:32).[114] As you have stated, you are guilty of fornication, and fornicators will not enter the Kingdom of God (see 1 Corinthians 6:9).[115]

<< 8. 'You shall not steal.' I've done this (slight kleptomaniac tendencies),[116] long ago, but have no desire to anymore, and I have not stolen anything in a long time. >>

You have admitted that you are a thief. Time doesn't forgive sin.

<< 9. 'You shall not bear false witness.' I have lied, and possibly have recently, which I must admit to. I don't enjoy lying, I can tell you that.>>

You are also a liar[117] (see Revelation 21:8).[118]

<< 10. 'You shall not covet.' I don't do this. I don't want a lot in my life when it comes to material goods. The things I want most can't be bought, and definitely can't be found at anyone's house. >>

Who of us can say that he has never desired something that belongs to someone else?

113 Matthew 5:26, 27.

114 "But I say unto you, That whosoever shall put away his wife, saving for the cause of fornication, causes her to commit adultery: and whosoever shall marry her that is divorced commits adultery" (Matthew 5:32).

115 "Do you not know that the unrighteous will not inherit the kingdom of God? Do not be deceived. Neither fornicators, nor idolaters, nor adulterers, nor homosexuals, nor sodomites, nor thieves, nor covetous, nor drunkards, nor revilers, nor extortioners will inherit the kingdom of God" (1 Corinthians 6:9, 10).

116 Dictionary: "An obsessive impulse to steal."

117 Who of us is not guilty of this sin?

118 Dictionary (n) *"One that tells lies."* "But the fearful, and unbelieving, and the abominable, and murderers, and whoremongers, and sorcerers, and idolaters, and all liars, shall have their part in the lake which burns with fire and brimstone: which is the second death" (Revelation 21:8).

119 "For whosoever shall keep the whole law, and yet offend in one point, he is guilty of all" (James 2:10).

120 Self-admitted.

The final nail in your coffin is that if you break one point of the Law, you are guilty of all (see James 2:10).[119] You don't have to break ten of man's laws to have the police after you; just one. California has a "three strikes and you're out" law. God has "One strike and you're out."

So you are in big trouble. God won't send you to Hell because you profess to be an atheist or because you don't believe in Jesus, but because you are an admitted liar. You are an admitted thief and a fornicator. (No wonder you deny God's existence.) That's just the sins you have acknowledged. It is because you are a liar[120] that I can't be sure you are telling me the truth when you profess to have always honored your parents, never coveted, never blasphemed and have kept the Sabbath holy. I don't want you to end up in Hell. Why do you think I keep pleading with you to be open to reason? God has made a way for you to be forgiven ... all you need is an open heart.

<< Well, I do enjoy sex, I admit, but it doesn't have to be a sin. Well, I can't see where exactly I love sin. Could you kindly point this out for me, Ray?>>

God created sex. The Bible says to enjoy the breasts of your wife[121] (not the lady down the street). There's nothing wrong with sex. God just said

90

that there are certain rules—like driving. Run red lights if you wish, but if you break the rules, you get hurt and you hurt other people (and you break the law). The same applies with fornication and adultery. If you break the rules, you get hurt—AIDS, VD, betrayal of trust within a marriage, guilt. Of course, many have dulled their consciences so that they don't hear their voices and feel guilt. That's like a man who takes the batteries out of his smoke detector because he doesn't like it disturbing his sleep.

The essence of sin is the "i" in the middle. "I" want to do "my" thing—God has no rights to my life! We act as though we are the center of the universe, answerable to nobody. We love sin and we hate the light of truth and righteousness. Check out TV, books, the movies, video stores, music, the tabloids—sex, blasphemy, unclean humor, adultery and violence. That sells, because we love the darkness of evil.[122]

* * *

How would you like it if I said this: "I know the real reason for your belief. It's your love of ignorance. Why don't you admit it, Ray? Your 'God'[123] and 'Bible' are just thin bushes you hide behind."

121 "Let your fountain be blessed: and rejoice with the wife of your youth. Let her be as the loving hind and pleasant roe; let her breasts satisfy you at all times; and be you ravished always with her love" (Proverbs 5:18, 19).

122 "And this is the condemnation, that the light has come into the world, and men loved darkness rather than light, because their deeds were evil. For everyone practicing evil hates the light and does not come to the light, lest his deeds should be exposed" (John 3:19-20).

123 Even though he is quoting me, it's good to see that he has given "God" and "Bible" capital letters for the first time.

91

That wouldn't concern me at all. I wouldn't see the need to try and justify myself because I know it's not true.

Now you know how I feel. Just because someone's different doesn't make them evil.

That's true.

Just because someone doesn't follow the same road as you do doesn't mean they're lost.

That's true. But if they are not following Jesus Christ, the Bible says that they are in darkness, "having their understanding darkened, being alienated from the life of God through the ignorance that is in them because of the blindness of their hearts" (Ephesians 4:18). That's about as lost as you can get.

Just because someone disagrees with you doesn't make them wrong.

True.

Ideas like these are what lead Hitler to kill the Jews. It's called hate, Ray— beware of it. It can mask itself as love, as well as a million other emotions.

To say that Hitler loved his enemies and did good to them is the epitome of ignorance. Hitler had no fear of

God. A wise man once said, "Most I fear God. Next, I fear him who fears Him not."

You are accusing me of the same things you are guilty of. You think that you are right, and because I disagree with your ideas, you think I am full of hatred ... a potential Nazi. Am I your enemy because I tell you the truth?

* * *

Why only 10 commandments? I think there should be more.

So does America. There are more than one million laws on the books.[124] Yet the Commandments are totally adequate. Do you remember the "essence" of the Commandments (see Mark 12:28-31): "You shall love your neighbor as yourself." If you do that, you won't lie to him, steal from him, kill him, hate him, or covet his car, his wife, his goods. You won't get drunk and hit your wife or child, torture anyone, believe in slavery (I believe in biblical "servants"—slaves in the old King James Version, but not our American heritage of the slavery of Africans), or have dishonest business practices (see Romans 13:9).[125]

[124] A slight underestimate. There are more than a million. In 1998 there were an estimated 35 million laws in the U.S.

[125] "For this, Thou shalt not commit adultery, Thou shalt not kill, Thou shalt not steal, Thou shalt not bear false witness, Thou shalt not covet; and if there be any other commandment, it is briefly comprehended in this saying, namely, Thou shalt love thy neighbor as thyself. Love works no ill to his neighbor: therefore love [is] the fulfilling of the law" (Romans 13:9, 10)

* * *

These are a few ... non-sins compared to sins that I thought of: A poor man

93

126 The reason that "atheist charities" is an oxymoron is probably that most atheists by definition believe in evolution. They therefore embrace Darwin's "survival of the fittest" philosophy, which has a condescending attitude towards (and at best barely tolerates) the less fortunate: "With savages, the weak in body and mind are soon eliminated; and those that survive commonly exhibit a vigorous state of health. We civilised men, on the other hand, do our utmost to check the process of elimination; we build asylums for the imbecile, the maimed and the sick; we institute poor laws; and our medical men exert their utmost skill to save the life of everyone to the last moment. There is reason to believe that vaccination has preserved thousands who, from a weak constitution, would formerly have succumbed to smallpox. Thus the weak members of civilised society propagate their kind.

"No one who has attended to the breeding of domestic animals will doubt that this must be highly injurious to the race of man. It is surprising how soon a want of care, or care wrongly directed, leads to the degeneration of a domestic race; but, excepting in the case of man himself, hardly anyone is so ignorant as to

stealing a loaf of bread to keep from starving—Sin.

<< You sure are a liberal. This is the reason given for the increase in crime in South Central Los Angeles. Haven't you heard of "work?'" >> I agree that these people should all find jobs, but if they don't, or if they can't, or if they're so disillusioned with the big city that they don't want to try, you'd just like them all to die off? Of course, I didn't say "unemployed," I said "poor." There are those with jobs from such poor families that they have to support everyone else, and a lot of times a roof over their head and some heat to keep them warm (things you obviously take for granted—I am guilty of it as well) takes them outside of their budget for food. Would you like these people to starve?

There will always be the poor and homeless, and they're not all bums who don't want to work. But, I bet you'd like to let them all die of starvation rather than steal a loaf of bread to eat. Do you agree with genocide? Obviously I'm taking your statement a little far here—I'd like them all to have jobs as much as you would, but if someone's going to starve, and they steal some food to eat, I WOULDN'T HOLD IT AGAINST THEM, unlike you and your god.

94

Instead of stealing, they could get free food from our church food ministry (we feed 2,500 families for the week, each Wednesday). Or they could go to the thousands of Christian charitable ministries around the country for free food and clothing.

Then again, they may like to try and find an atheist charitable organization and get free food and clothing from them. There may be one ... somewhere. Perhaps you could enlighten me in that respect. I guess I must be ignorant.[126]

* * *

<< I find it interesting when you use bad language. It shows me that I'm rocking your boat a little.>>[127] I suppose you mean "(expletive)." Well, "bad language" is subjective.

Also, of course you're rocking my boat—you made me out to be another one of those excuse-making freaks who blames everyone but themselves. First of all, who am I blaming? No one. I happily accept full responsibility for not believing—I'm proud of being an atheist.[128]

It may not be a conscious choice, but it's still part of my personality, and thus I am completely to blame. But, I don't see the need to blame myself or anyone else for not believing—I

allow his worst animals to breed.

"The aid which we feel impelled to give to the helpless is mainly an incidental result of the instinct of sympathy, which was originally acquired as part of the social instincts, but subsequently rendered in the manner previously indicated more tender and more widely diffused. Nor can we check our sympathy, even without deterioration in the noblest part of our nature ... We must, therefore, bear the undoubtedly bad effects of the weak surviving and propagating their kind." *The Descent of Man* (2nd Ed., pp. 133–134, 1887).

127 Some of our correspondence was unfortunately lost.

128 "Science can only be created by those who are thoroughly imbued with the aspiration toward truth and understanding. This source of feeling, however, springs from the sphere of religion. To this there also belongs the faith in the possibility that the regulations valid for the world of existence are rational, that is, comprehensible to reason. I cannot conceive of a genuine scientist without that profound faith."
– Albert Einstein

actually don't see any problem with it. Like I said, I'm proud to be called an atheist.

But, that stands apart from the FACT that BELIEF IS NOT A CHOICE. Try to dispute that, and I'll forward your email to about 7 psychologists, 4 doctors and 8 psychiatrists, all of differing religions (probably—never bothered to ask), who will each tell you just how and why belief is not a conscious choice that one can make. Belief is a part of your personal makeup.

<< The word "belief" in the Bible means "to trust.">> That's fine, I'll accept that. To keep everything clear, when I mean "believe," I'll say "believe," and when I mean "trust," I'll say "trust," alright?

This means that god punishes those who do not trust in him—not because they didn't trust in his power, but because they transgressed his law (ala your parachute analogy).

But, if someone honestly doesn't believe it (like me), how can they be expected to trust in his power? You're asking me to jump out of that plane, you're asking me to trust in this parachute of yours, but how am I supposed to believe anyone who says that this parachute will actually open?

The only thing that tells me the parachute works is a parachute manual which is thousands of years old and could very well be completely false. How's that for an analogy?

I don't believe anything you say. You are a liar. You are not worthy of my trust. You are devious, underhanded, and insidious.

How would that make you feel if I said that about you (even though you have admitted these things)? That's what you are saying when you don't believe God's "exceedingly great and precious promises." "He that believes not God has made Him a liar" (1 John 5:10, 11).

I know that this fact won't concern you at all. You hold even the thought of God in contempt. You never even bother to give His name a capital and yet I have noticed that you have given your god (Satan) capitals a number of times.

* * *

<< I suppose you think murderers shouldn't be punished. Let me know your thoughts about that. >> I'm an "eye for an eye" kind of person when it comes to justice. I'd like to see cold-blooded killers who kill with malicious intent to get exactly what they gave,

every last one of them. I bet crime rates would be a lot lower with that kind of justice system in place.

But, Ray, you didn't answer my question—What is the purpose of hell? There is no comparing theistic punishment with civil punishment. Criminals are put into jail for the good of society, because they pose a threat. So then, what is hell for? Do they have to burn for the good of everyone in heaven? Is it in their best interest to know that there are billions of souls being tortured cruelly every second for eternity? The good of society in heaven would be to not allow sinners, that is understandable, but what's the purpose of torturing them FOREVER? It's not justice. It's just sick. When god could simply "uncreate" (for lack of a better term) their consciousness and dispose of it mercifully, with no hard feelings either way, why would he choose to have them punished?

I think it is you who has evaded the question.

It's nice to hear you quote the Bible in context. Most unsaved people think, "An eye for an eye" has something to do with personal retribution, when it is speaking of restitution in civil justice.

However, like most in the world, you have misunderstood the chief purpose of justice. A murderer doesn't go to

prison primarily to protect society from future murders. He goes to prison because he took someone's life. He murdered another human being. He is there for punishment ... for retribution.

God's punishment isn't to "reform the criminal" (which is what many nowadays think it's for), and it's not primarily to protect the innocent from future crimes. Hell is punishment for sin. Death is a "wage" (see Romans 6:23).[129] We earn it. I hope this makes sense. Yours faithfully, Ray

129 "For the wages of sin is death; but the gift of God is eternal life through Jesus Christ our Lord" (Romans 6:23).

* * *

This is what I was afraid of. That's why I put this little disclaimer in, did you read it? "Keep in mind that what I name I name from my own beliefs. In your beliefs, everything has a maker, so in your mind, I can't name anything."

How do you expect me to answer you to your satisfaction? Oh, by the way, those things I mentioned, they weren't made by god, because there is no god. Put that statement next to yours, and look at them. Neither is any more valid because they are just assertions, nothing more.

James. I wonder if you would question me if I said, "There are no diamonds in Missouri. Not one. Don't even bother checking. Believe me, I know." I think you would have the right to question my sanity. The only possible way I could know that there are no diamonds in your entire state, is to know everything. I would need to know what's in the heart of every rock—what's deep beneath the crust of the earth; what's in every ear, nose, on every hand, and in every store. If there was just one diamond in Missouri, then my statement is fallacious ... a lie. I'm either incredibly arrogant, unbelievably egocentric (thinking I am omniscient), or I am a fool who has no depth of thought.

Before you say the same applies to someone who says, "There are diamonds in Missouri"—a child doesn't need all knowledge to say, "My mother has two real diamonds in her wedding ring." All he needs is the simple knowledge that his mother has diamonds in the ring. The same applies with those who have had a genuine encounter with their Creator, which I had in 1972.

* * *

The statement "There is no God" can only be said by Someone Who has omniscience ... sorry James, you are not He.

What I think you are talking about here is what's called "Pascal's Wager," which is a[130] fallacious argument stating that it is a "better bet" to believe in a god than to not. This is, of course, assuming that one can simply choose their belief, which one can not.

<< Yet you have everything to gain if what I say is true. >> I know that. If I only I could believe you were right. But, I can't.

Won't (see Psalm 10:4).[131]

<< Won't. (see Psalm 10:4). >> No, "CAN'T." I think I know my mind better than you and your bible.

He that trusts his own heart is a fool (see Proverbs 28:26). Won't.

* * *

I got this from a friend today; thought you would like it: Imagine an Englishman, a Frenchman, a Chinese and an Indonesian all looking at a cup. The Englishman says, "That is a cup." The Frenchman answers, "No it's not. It's a tasse." The Chinese comments, "You are both wrong. It's a pei." And the Indonesian laughs at the others and says, "What a fool you are. It's a cawan." The Englishman gets a dictionary and shows it to the others, saying, "I can prove that it is a cup. My dictionary says so." "Then your

130 Pascal was a seventeenth-century scientist who majored in physics, and mathematics—especially "probability theory." He is credited with inventing the world's first working computer, vacuum cleaner, and public transportation system. This is his famous wager: "Who then will condemn Christians for being unable to give rational grounds for their belief ... They declare that it is folly, stultitiam, in expounding it to the world, and then you complain that they do not prove it ...

"Let us examine this point, and let us say: 'Either God is or He is not.' But to which view shall we be inclined? Reason cannot decide this question. Infinite chaos separates us. At the far end of this infinite distance, a coin is being spun which will come down heads or tails. How will you wager? Reason cannot make you choose either, reason cannot prove either wrong.

"Do not then condemn as wrong those who have made a choice, for you know nothing about it. 'No, but I will condemn them not for having made this particular choice, for, although the one who calls heads and the other one are equally at fault, that fact is that they are both at fault: the right thing is not to wager at all.'

"Yes, but you must wager. There is no choice,

you are already committed. Which will you choose then? Let us see: since a choice must be made, let us see which offers you the least interest. You have two things to lose: the true and the good; and two things to stake: your reason and your will, your knowledge and your happiness; and your nature has two things to avoid: error and wretchedness. Since you must necessarily choose, your reason is no more affronted by choosing one rather than the other. That is one point cleared up. But your happiness? Let us weigh up the gain and the loss involved in calling heads that God exists. Let us assess the two cases: if you win, you win everything. If you lose, you lose nothing. Do not hesitate then; wager that he does exist. That is wonderful. Yes, I must wager, but perhaps I am wagering too much. Let us see: since there is an equal chance of gain and loss, if you stood to win only two lives for one, you could still wager. But supposing you stood to win three? ...

"I tell you that you will gain even in this life, and that at every step you take along this road you will see that your gain is so certain and your risk so negligible that in the end you will realize that you have wagered on something certain and

dictionary is wrong," says the Frenchman "because my dictionary clearly says it is a tasse." The Chinese scoffs at them. "My dictionary is thousands of years older than yours, so my dictionary must be right. And besides, more people speak Chinese than any other language, so it must be pei." While they are squabbling and arguing with each other, a Buddhist comes up and drinks from the cup. After he has drunk, he says to the others, "Whether you call it a cup, a tasse, a pei or a cawan, the purpose of the cup is to be used. Stop arguing and drink, stop squabbling and refresh your thirst." This is the Buddhist attitude to other religions.

An atheist comes in, looks at the cup and says, "There is no cup."

* * *

James. I received the Christmas gift today.[132] **It made me smile. I couldn't help but think of the movie "Ben Hur"—where Judah Ben-Hur gave a precious knife to his enemy (not that we are enemies). Both his gift and yours were "exquisitely appropriate."**

Are you trying to stir me up? Well, if you are, you have! How could you believe that each painting in the book had no painter? How could you (in your right mind) believe that the book had no printer—it merely happened by

accident ... over trillions of years. Give me a break. There is obviously an ulterior motive for such intellectual suicide.

I get given many books—but this one is special because of who gave it to me.

Thank you.

God bless, Ray

Post Script

In 2005, I made a number of unsuccessful attempts to contact James. Perhaps he came into some money and was able to afford to leave the United States. In one of his letters he said, "Okay, first of all the American justice system is not in any way equal to god's justice—I have enough distaste for the American way altogether that I want to move to another country as soon as I can afford it—and I MEAN that!"

infinite for which you have paid nothing." (From *Christianity for Modern Pagans*, Peter Kreeft, Ignatius)

131 "The wicked, through the pride of his countenance, will not seek after God: God is not in all his thoughts" (Psalm 10:4).

132 It was a beautiful book of paintings, *Glory of Creation* by Thomas Kinkade. He enclosed a card, which said, "Ray—Warmest Holiday Wishes To You And Yours," and then signed his name (in caps)

Epilogue

If you are a Christian, you may like to consider writing your own emails to the unsaved. Get on the Internet and type in the search words "atheist," "skeptic," "religious hypocrisy," "humanist," or "freethinker." Look for forums, email addresses, articles, etc., and it won't be long until you find an email address of someone who is anti-Christian. Then email them saying something like, "Dear James. I was surfing the Net, saw your interesting emails about religious hypocrisy, and thought, 'What has all this got to do with the fact that James will stand before God on Judgment Day (whether he believes in Him or not) and give an account of his life—as will all religious pretenders.' I trust you are well. Sincerely, (your name)."

If you are asked a difficult question, go to www.livingwaters.com and click on "Free Evangelism Resources," then "Free Answers Tool." There you will find answers to one hundred of the most common questions and objections to the Christian faith. These can be freely cut and pasted into your emails.

Always show respect and patience. Read your replies through a few times prayerfully before you send them, to make sure they are filled with grace. It won't be long until you excitedly open your email, looking for replies from your atheist friend.

APPENDIX

1. Only in recent years has science discovered that everything we see is composed of invisible atoms. Here, Scripture tells us that the "things which are seen were not made of things which do appear" (Hebrews 11:3).

2. Medical science has only recently discovered that blood-clotting in a newborn reaches its peak on the eighth day, then drops. The Bible consistently says that a baby must be circumcised on the eighth day. [See Phillippians 3:3.]

3. At a time when it was believed that the earth sat on a large animal or a giant (1500 B.C.), the Bible spoke of the earth's free float in space: "He ... hangs the earth upon nothing" (Job 26:7).

4. The prophet Isaiah also tells us that the earth is round: "It is he that sits upon the circle of the earth" (Isaiah 40:22). This is not a reference to a flat disk, as some skeptics maintain, but to a sphere. Secular man discovered this 2,400 years later. At a time when science believed that the earth was flat, it was Scripture that inspired Christopher Columbus to sail around the world.

5. God told Job in 1500 B.C.: "Can you send lightnings, that they may go, and say to you, Here we are?" (Job 38:35). The Bible here is making what appears to be a scientifically ludicrous statement—that light can be *sent*, and then manifest itself in speech. But did you know that radio waves travel at the speed of light? This is why you can have *instantaneous* wireless communication with someone on the other side of the earth. Science didn't discover this until 1864 when "British scientist James Clerk Maxwell suggested that electricity andlight waves were two forms of the same thing" (*Modern Century Illustrated Encyclopedia*).

6. Job 38:19 asks, "Where is the way where light dwells?" Modern man has only recently discovered that light (electromagnetic radiation) has a "way," traveling at 186,000 miles per second.

7. Science has discovered that stars emit radio waves, which are received on earth as a high pitch. God mentioned this in Job 38:7: "When the morning stars sang together ..."

8. "Most cosmologists (scientists who study the structures and evolution of the universe) agree that the Genesis account of creation, in imagining an initial void, may be uncannilyclose to the truth" (*Time*, December 1976).

9. Solomon described a "cycle" of air currents 2,000 years before scientists "discovered" them. "The wind goes toward the south, and turns about unto the north; it whirls about continually, and the wind returns again according to his circuits" (Ecclesiastes 1:6).

10. Science expresses the universe in five terms: time, space, matter, power, and motion. Genesis 1:1,2 revealed such truths to the Hebrews in 1450 B.C.: "In the beginning [*time*] God created [*power*] the heaven [*space*] and the earth [*matter*] ... And the Spirit of God moved [*motion*] upon the face of the waters." The first thing God tells man is that He controls of all aspects of the universe.

11. The great biological truth concerning the importance of blood in our body's mechanism has been fully comprehended only in recent years. Up until 120 years ago, sick people were "bled," and many died because of the practice. If you lose

your blood, you lose your life. Yet Leviticus 17:11, written 3,000 years ago, declared that blood is the source of life: "For the life of the flesh is in the blood."

12. *Encyclopedia Britannica* documents that in 1845, a young doctor in Vienna named Dr. Ignaz Semmelweis was horrified at the terrible death rate of women who gave birth in hospitals. As many as 30 percent died after giving birth. Semmelweis noted that doctors would examine the bodies of patients who died, then, without washing their hands, go straight to the next ward and examine expectant mothers. This was their normal practice, because the presence of microscopic diseases was unknown. Semmelweis insisted that doctors wash their hands before examinations, and the death rate immediately dropped to 2 percent. Look at the specific instructions God gave His people for when they encounter disease: "And when he that has an issue is cleansed of his issue; then he shall number to himself seven days for his cleansing, and wash his clothes, and bathe his flesh in running water, and shall be clean" (Leviticus 15:13). Until recent years, doctors washed their hands in a bowl of water, leaving invisible germs on their hands. However, the Bible says specifically to wash hands under "running water."

13. Luke 17:34–36 says the Second Coming of Jesus Christ will occur while some are asleep at night and others are working at daytime activities in the field. This is a clear indication of a revolving earth, with day and night at the same time.

14. "During the devastating Black Death of the fourteenth century, patients who were sick or dead were kept in the same rooms as the rest of the family. People often wondered why the disease was affecting so many people at one time. They attributed these epidemics to 'bad air' or 'evil spirits.' However, careful attention to the medical commands of God as revealed in Leviticus would have saved untold millions of lives. Arturo Castiglione wrote about the overwhelming importance of this biblical medical law: 'The laws against leprosy in Leviticus 13 may be regarded as the first model of sanitary legislation.' (*A History of Medicine*)" Grant R. Jeffery, *The Signature of God*. With all these truths revealed in Scripture, how could a thinking person deny that the Bible is supernatural in origin? There is no other book in any of the world's religions (*Vedas, Bhagavad-Gita, Koran, Book of Mormon*, etc.) that contains scientific truth. In fact, they contain statements that are clearly unscientific. Hank Hanegraaff said, "Faith in Christ is not some blind leap into a dark chasm, but a faith based on established evidence." (From *The Evidence Bible*)

Don't Miss the New

Intelligent Design
vs.
EVOLUTION

Board Game

For more information about Ray Comfort,
visit www.livingwaters.com,
call 800-437-1893, or write to:
Living Waters Publications
P.O. Box 1172
Bellflower, CA 90706

"The Way of the Master"
Evidence Bible

Prove God's existence. Answer 100 common objections to Christianity. Show the Bible's supernatural origin. This unique study Bible includes wisdom from the foremost Christian leaders of yesterday and today such as Charles Spurgeon, D.L. Moody, John Wesley, Charles Finney, George Whitefield, Billy Graham, Dr. Bill Bright, John MacArthur, and R.C. Sproul.

Complete Bible available in
• Hardback
• Leather-bound (black or burgundy)
• Paperback

New Testament, Proverbs & Pslams
    available in
• Paperback
• Black leather-bound pocket editon

AVAILABLE AT FINE CHRISTIAN BOOKSTORES

More **Bridge-Logos** Titles
from Ray Comfort

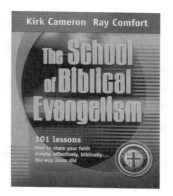

The School of Biblical Evangelism
In this comprehensive study course, you will learn how to share our faith simply, effectively, and biblically … the way Jesus did. Discover the God-given evangelistic tools that will enable you to confidently talk about the Savior.

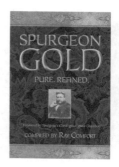

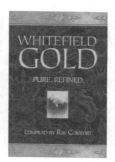

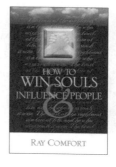

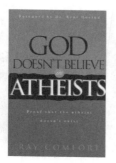